ADVANCE PRAISE FOR
WISDOM OF THE BODY

Wisdom of the Body is a mirror. each chapter, but it is not the surfa You see the deeper self, the hidder your attitudes toward body, sexua ......macy. In this way, reading this book is a journey of discovery. The proper response is not to praise it extravagantly, but to say thank you.

> —John Shea, author of *Gospel Light: Jesus Stories for Spiritual Consciousness* and *Stories of God*

The Whiteheads' new interdisciplinary *Wisdom of the Body* . . . presents us with genuine Gospel wisdom for today. The book offers thoughtful reflection on the sensitive issues that engage us all.

> —Anne Carr, Professor of Theology, The University of Chicago

In *Wisdom of the Body,* Evelyn and James Whitehead write with wisdom and excitement as they tell our stories of bodily alienation and healing and invite us . . . toward greater wholeness and integration in our God-given sexuality.

> —Rev. James Schexnayder, National Association of Catholic Diocesan Lesbian and Gay Ministries.

The Whiteheads are among only a few voices today showing the intimate and necessary connection between sexuality and spirituality . . . their focus on the gendered dimensions of our sexuality provides for expanded appreciation of our unique emotional and relational development.

> —Paul Giblin, Institute of Pastoral Studies, Loyola University Chicago

WISDOM OF THE BODY

Wisdom of the Body

Making Sense of Our Sexuality

Evelyn Eaton Whitehead
&
James D. Whitehead

A Crossroad Faith and Formation Book
The Crossroad Publishing Company
New York

The Crossroad Publishing Company
481 Eighth Avenue, New York, NY 10001

Printed in the United States of America

Library of Congress Cataloging-in-Publication Data

Whitehead, Evelyn Eaton.
    Wisdom of the body : making sense of our sexuality / Evelyn
Eaton Whitehead & James D. Whitehead.
        p.   cm.
    Includes bibliographical references.
    ISBN 0-8245-1954-X (alk. paper)
    1. Sex—Religious aspects—Catholic Church. I. Whitehead, James
D. II. Title.
BX1795.S48 W48 2001
233'.5--dc21

                                                    2001001504

        3   4   5   6   7   8   9   10

For
James R. Zullo
Friend and Colleague

Contents

Preface

I T WAS THE WORST OF TIMES, it was the best of times. Over a decade ago when our book *A Sense of Sexuality* first appeared, these sentiments seemed an accurate description. Promiscuity and pornography were prevalent in U.S. culture. Domestic violence and sexual addictions were on the rise. Charges of sexual abuse were leveled against leaders in both church and society. But this distress was not all. In the midst of these negative realities, sometimes prompted by them, people of faith were finding their voice.

In faith communities and religious congregations, in the protected settings of pastoral counseling and spiritual care, in candid discussions among colleagues and friends, in publications and public debate—Christians gained confidence to speak the truth about their experience of sexuality.

We were privileged to be part of these conversations, often in the good company of our colleague, psychologist James R. Zullo. Such conversations, and the hard-won wisdom they voiced, have shaped our understanding of sexuality, of spirituality, and of their intimate connection in Christian living.

These conversations continue. And here in *Wisdom of the Body* we attempt again to explore the Christian sense of sexuality, drawing on theological resources, psychological and social research, and the communal wisdom of Christian lives. This book retains several chapters from Part 1, "The Possibilities," and Part 3, "The Arenas of Intimacy," in *A Sense of Sexuality.* Each of these chapters has been modified slightly to reflect developments over the past decade. Three new chapters expand our earlier discussion of gender by considering femininity, masculinity, and the complicated question of the differences (real and imagined) between men and women. We offer a new chapter on homosexuality as well. The "Additional Resources" listing at the end of each chapter is completely updated to reflect the wealth of valuable new material now available.

With our colleagues at Crossroad Publishing Company, we see *Wisdom of the Body* as the first of two volumes. In the second—tentatively entitled *The Virtues of Eros*—we will expand the themes of passion and pleasure that we treated in *A Sense of Sexuality,* in a new discussion of the practices that shape Christian living.

A special note of thanks is due here to Steve Erspamer, SM, the multitalented artist based in St. Louis, Missouri. His line drawing "The Marriage of Eros and Grace" was commissioned by the Aquinas Institute of Theology for the Fifteenth Annual Aquinas Lecture in 1996, which we were honored to present. We are grateful to Steve for granting permission for his work to appear on the cover of our book.

This book, the fruit of many conversations, we dedicate to our chief conversation partner, James Zullo. Jim is a psychologist, teacher, therapist, religious brother, mentor to many, friend and colleague to us. With appreciation and affection, we salute him—once again.

E.E.W. & J. D. W.
Easter 2001

Part One

Exploring the Wisdom of the Body

WE ARE THE BODY OF CHRIST. What are the erotic possibilities of the body Christian? What shall we make of our sexuality? In Part 1 we attempt to give voice to the wisdom of Christian experience and Christian tradition in their testimony that sex is good, sex is mysterious, and sex makes promises.

The Christian vision expands the scope of love. The gospel brings good news for the body, rescuing sexuality from narrow understandings that limit *eros* to genital activity. And the robust virtue of intimacy equips us for the wider challenges of love and work.

1

Making Sense of Sexuality

C HRISTIANS HAVE A SENSE OF SEXUALITY. It is a communal wisdom, rooted in the graciousness of God's creation and shaped by the witness of Jesus' life. For two thousand years Christians have struggled to believe the good news of the Gospels—that God is among us, within us. Our bodies are not barriers to grace. If we could truly accept this, then we would know God even in the ambiguous delights of our sexuality.

After Jesus died and was raised, his friends sensed that he was still present in their gatherings. "Now you together are the body of Christ" (1 Corinthians 12:27), Paul proclaimed. As the body of Christ, the Christian community carries a shared wisdom about sex and love, a wisdom born of our efforts to have God's word shape our sexuality. This communal wisdom, which recognizes that we are accountable to one another and to the gospel, is not limited to formal pronouncements and received doctrines. Rooted in the daily practical decisions through which we try to love well, this fragile wisdom emerges from our frequent failures and our continuing hopes.

In this book we attempt to give voice to the wisdom of the body. We begin this chapter with four stories of sexual Christians. Then we name the yearning heard in these stories. Finally, we will look again at the image of the body of Christ. We view this metaphor in terms of an emerging wisdom about sexuality, a wisdom to which contemporary believers bear witness in their lives.

Christians and Their Sexuality:
Four Portraits

Julie and I were married nineteen years ago yesterday. It seems more like ten years, but our three teenagers remind us that it is almost twenty. The weekend retreat announced in the parish bulletin last month looked like an opportunity to catch our breath and relax. We thought the time away would be a good chance for us to unwind. We thought that until we heard the question from the leader-couple: "What was the biggest crisis in your marriage?"

We both knew the answer to this question but were reluctant to return to "the scene of the crime." It wasn't a dramatic crisis like alcoholism or sexual infidelity, but it was still very painful. Five years ago, on a very snowy night, we finally admitted that we had lost touch with each other. Our absorption in two jobs and three children had aided this gradual separation and had also disguised it. We admitted that we hardly really talked to one another; we got angry with each other for no apparent reason. We didn't share much of anything; we didn't even make love anymore. To outsiders we may have looked like a wonderful family, but underneath our marriage was dying.

We started seeing a good marriage counselor and began slowly to find our way back together. Old and stubborn habits, especially Julie's sarcasm and my tendency to withdraw, needed to be broken. We began to learn again how to talk about our feelings and fears, without punishing each other. We began to remember to thank each other for little things, to take the time to express affection. As we got to know each other again we were surprised how much we had changed over nineteen years. We hadn't noticed each other changing, hadn't allowed for it. With the counselor we began to discover what fidelity means for us: to stay in touch, to nurture the commitment we have—not just for our children but for us as partners.

Some wounds remain from that crisis five years ago. But today we enjoy being together. We still have arguments but they are aboveboard and direct, and we find our way through them without much damage. We even look forward to the days ahead when our three children have left home and we are on our own again. The weekend retreat was no picnic, but it was very good for us. It wasn't relaxing, but it was energizing. We are grateful for the crisis; it got our attention and started us on the task of rebuilding our love.

I joined a religious community of sisters twenty-six years ago because I wanted to be a teacher and to become holy. In our early training program we were instructed not to form special friendships. As vowed religious, we were to love everyone, but not to show any particular affection for another individual. In the years that followed this early training (I entered the novitiate when I was twenty), I learned to be very restrained in my emotions. I was seeking a deep relationship with Jesus Christ, and I saw the love of others as a hindrance to this goal. Celibacy protected me on this solitary journey.

For a dozen or more years I seemed to "forget" my body and my emotions. I don't think I hated my body; I just ignored it and the emotions that resided within it. When I fell in love at age thirty-eight, this well-constructed world disintegrated. Something both terrible and wonderful was happening: I was losing the control that had become the cornerstone of my religious life. I was being introduced to a very different God—a livelier, more affectionate, (dare I say it?) more feminine God.

With the crash of my well-protected lifestyle, I thought that my religious and celibate vocation was over. In time I found that it was not ending, but only changing. Now I have three very close friends with whom I delight in sharing my heart. With my dearest friend I have been learning—with some awkwardness—how to express affection in ways that respect my vow of celibacy. And I have, happily, become more a friend of my own body—this wonderful, lovely, neglected part of myself. I listen with less panic to its stirring, whether of anger or sexuality; I pay more attention to its hints about fatigue and loneliness. Celibacy is no longer just a way for me to hide from contact. I am aware in deeper ways how this commitment fits me, how my celibacy is a part of my own way of loving well. The affection of friends sustains me on days when I sorely miss being married and having children. In my teaching I feel fruitful. I will never be a parent, but I give thanks for the new life to which my ministry contributes. And I am most grateful for the affection that is such an exciting part of my life these days.

Dear Alice,

That was such a good talk on the phone last night. Your tough questions rattled me, but in a good way. When I woke this morning our conversation was continuing in my head. Here are some of my tentative responses.

I am able to say, for the first time, that I may not marry. I have been defensive about this until just recently; I think this was part of my curtness toward you last night. I had always assumed I would marry (don't all good girls?), even as I resisted my parents' growing pressure for me to "meet someone nice and settle down." I am becoming more comfortable with myself as unmarried. I like my life and feel that I can make a real contribution as I am. I really don't feel "incomplete."

What I miss most is any support for being single. At work I am seen as either a threat or someone to "hit on." Our parish does not seem much interested in anyone who is not married. It lavishes attention on the teenagers and is doing more for family life. Often I feel not only left out, but that I am, in some way, dangerous. Surely people don't think I am going to seduce someone's husband or some poor, defenseless youth! (Could they believe that I am really not all that interested?)

As a Catholic I find myself asking the question: What does it mean to be single and sexual? I have not chosen a celibate life. But I do not "sleep around." Is there any ground between these extremes of abstinence and promiscuity? Where can Catholics even have this conversation? Sex is such an all-or-nothing proposition for us. There may be some wisdom in this approach for teenagers (I'm not even sure that's true!) but what about mature adults?

It seems that as a relationship deepens, questions of sexual sharing arise as a natural part of this growth. In my experience this is neither irresponsible nor sinful. I suspect that many single Catholics have these experiences; my regret is that no one speaks about it. Will this ever change?

Thanks for listening to my ramblings. Call or write when you can.

Love,
Sue

Last Christmas we received the worst possible surprise: our son Nicholas told us he is gay. Our response sounds funny now, but his father and I tried to talk him out of it! Surely he was mistaken! Not our son! When Nick assured us that he had been aware of his sexual orientation since junior high school, we refused to believe him. There was a terrible scene and our anger drove him out. For a week a thick cloud hung over the house. The two of us spent all our energy avoiding the topic. Finally we couldn't stand it anymore. We went to our good friend at the parish, Sister Ann.

When we gave our embarrassing news, Ann was neither astonished nor alarmed. We were so relieved that we spent the next hour expressing all our feelings of dismay. When we had finished, Ann asked a simple question: "How is Nick different now that you know he is gay?" This confused us both: everything is different! But Ann pushed on: "Is Nick promiscuous?" No. "Is he selfish, immature, turned in on himself?" No. "Then what is different?" We weren't sure. This was all we could handle that day. As we left, we carried the odd realization that Nick was still the same lovable person—our son—even if he is this new and terrible thing called "homosexual."

The next week Sister Ann had another question for us: "What do you most regret about Nick being gay?" My husband regretted that his son was committing serious sins. My regret was that he would not marry "a nice girl" and have a family. As we talked, we had to admit a third regret: we were ashamed of what our friends and neighbors would think. We would be looked down on by them because we had failed as parents.

At our third meeting Sister Ann asked another question: "What do you most want for Nick?" At last, an easy question! We both want him to be happy, to have a good life. It is hard to say, but we want him to find love. Beyond that Ann helped us name some other wants: that Nick would "make us proud," that he would give us grandchildren. It wasn't until then that we saw we want these things for ourselves more than for Nick.

All these questions and answers happened a year ago. This Christmas Nick introduced us to his friend, William. What are we to think? We love Nick so much but are still so confused about his life. How can we best love him?

The Yearning

In these stories of Christian lives we hear a yearning. These voices long for a more optimistic and generous view of our sexual lives. The longing takes shape in three hopes. First, we hope to recover the sense of our sexuality as a gift. As Christians, we believe that sexuality is part of the original blessing of creation; for this we are grateful. We give thanks for our own lives—a gift from our parents' generous sexual love. We give thanks for the gift of those who share with us love's delights. We give thanks for the gift of fruitfulness (our children and our other "works of love") that comes to be through our passion. All these gifts surprise and humble us, for we have not earned them, nor are they under our control.

But another powerful emotion often usurps the place of gratitude for sexuality. Guilt insinuates itself into our heart. We know guilt can be a valuable and necessary response, "the guardian of our goodness," as psychologist Willard Gaylin says. We know that genuine guilt arouses the heart, warning us of wounds for which we are responsible. We know this emotion can serve our sexuality—reaffirming our values, protecting our commitments, alerting us to the selfishness that can too easily infect our lives. But this powerful emotion often goes astray, crippling our ability to express affection and turning us away from the risks of sexual love. When this happens, guilt drives out gratitude. Obsessed with sexual temptations, we become absorbed in our own wretchedness. Hounded by guilt, we forget to be grateful for the gift of sexuality. Garrison Keillor's character in *Lake Wobegone Days* speaks for many Christians as he describes his religious upbringing with bitter humor:

> You have taught me to feel shame and disgust about my body, so that I am afraid to clear my throat or blow my nose. . . . You taught me an indecent fear of sexuality. I'm not sure I have any left underneath this baked-on crust of shame and disgust. . . . A year ago a friend offered to give me a backrub. I declined vociferously. You did this to me.

A genuinely Christian response to sexuality insists that gratitude precede guilt. But here a painful realization dawns: religious institutions have sometimes used guilt as a tool to manage the faithful. Through guilt, institutions exercise control: they tell us what is shameful, what is sinful, what merits punishment. So in our sexual lives—where control seems so important—these institutions, perhaps inevitably, stress guilt more strenuously than gratitude. Unfortunately such an approach produces a peculiar brand of Christian: one who avoids contact with other people, lest they become an occasion of sin; one who mistrusts pleasure because it threatens the loss of total control.

The yearning among many Christians today is for a reversal of these religious sentiments: to recover the priority of gratitude in our sexual lives and to put genuine guilt into a secondary role.

The second hope is for a more incarnational attitude toward sexuality. The abstract word *Incarnation* has at its core a wonderfully concrete meaning: flesh. Christians hope for a spirituality of sexuality that is more comfortable with the flesh.

Christian teachings on sexuality have become abstract and idealistic. Official statements about marriage, for example, compare this relationship to the exalted union of Christ and the church, but often remain silent about the important daily dynamics of love and conflict. At times Christian spirituality was more than abstract; it was hostile to the body and sexuality. Spiritual guides in our religious tradition often suggested that holiness and sexuality were incompatible; sexual arousal was essentially selfish; the human body, a site of sinfulness, was to be punished and subdued. It was not to be befriended but mastered. A dualism of body and soul, flesh and spirit sapped the best convictions of our faith.

All this was heresy, of course. But it powerfully influenced centuries of Christian spirituality. What Christians hope for today is a return to the best belief of the Incarnation: in the flesh we meet God; in our bodies the power of God stirs; our sexuality is an ordinary medium through which God's love moves to touch, to create, to heal.

Christians have a third hope that springs from their longing. They want to appreciate the positive links between pleasure and commitment. Religious writers have often portrayed these two aspects of our sexual lives as antagonists. A virtuous life seemed to demand an either/or choice: either we selfishly pursue pleasure or we settle down to a responsible, if arid, adult life. Commitment and duty appeared incompatible with pleasure and delight.

In such a standoff, both sides suffered. We came to understand commitment as drab and unexciting; we understood physical lovemaking as only *taking* pleasure, not sharing or giving delight. To such a selfish act we gave the sinister name "concupiscence." In this view, heaven became the proper place for pleasure. Through the centuries, the mystics delighted in describing union with God in the most erotic imagery. This beautiful poetry was often interpreted to mean that pleasure and delight have little place in this world.

Christians today give witness to another wisdom: in lovemaking, couples learn to both give and receive pleasure. The erotic life is about much more than "taking" pleasure—in its rapacious and selfish meanings. Lovemaking invites us into a rhythm of pleasuring and being pleasured—as does any lasting experience of mutuality. This combination of activity and receptivity, of control and letting go, requires a genuine discipline. As Catholic philosopher Dick Westley observes: "The fact is that sexual activity, when it is truly lovemaking and the work of the spirit, is the antithesis of self-indulgence. It is the height of asceticism." At the core of sexual love, this discipline links pleasure to both responsibility and fruitfulness.

A Bodily Wisdom

Today the body Christian wants to reclaim the original optimism of the Incarnation—God's confidence in the body and its passionate hopes. This book is part of that effort. In the chapters that follow we explore the connections between the experience of sexuality and the life of faith. In pursuit of a spirituality of sexuality, we give special attention to three sources: Christian tradition, the culture in which we live, and the experience of Christians today.

Most of us carry our religious heritage as a rich and dense storehouse; energizing values and lingering guilt abide there together. Images abound: God as a loving parent, God as an unforgiving judge, our bodies as temples of the Holy Spirit, our bodies as shameful and inherently sinful. Christian tradition holds an especially ambiguous set of images and values about sexuality. The complexity starts in the book of Genesis. Having created woman and man as sexual companions, God judges that this creation is good! This compelling account of a couple delighting in one another and in the presence of God moves us all. It speaks of a promise and a hope—a hope realized in our own experience in those extraordinary moments of uncovering ourselves to one another in love. In such moments, however rare, we find a more than genital pleasure in the discovery of the goodness of life.

But in this same story, another view of sexuality insinuates itself. The failure of this couple—some terrible, original mistake that seems necessary to account for the deep and continuous ways men and women fail themselves and one another—appears to be connected in some way with sexuality. Although Genesis describes this original sin as disobedience, the original couple feel its results in their sexual bodies. After their sin, the couple's punishment is alienation—from God (they are driven from the garden), from one another (they are suddenly aware of their nakedness), and from an easy delight in their bodies (man's work will be "by the sweat of his brow" and women will bear children "in anguish").

The complexity of religious attitudes toward sexuality is discovered again in the Christian tradition. The image of the Incarnation itself reveals a central ambiguity concerning the meaning and value of sex. God is made flesh, becomes embodied as a sexual person like us. In this event our bodies too are blessed and reaffirmed in their holiness. Yet this enfleshing of God's son was interpreted in the early Christian centuries as having happened asexually. Growing suspicious of sexuality under the increasing influence of the Greek world, the early church decreed that God became human but not through a genital act. For many Christians today, this interpretation drains the Incarnation of its promise.

The Christian tradition is more than a sacred and unchanging reservoir of revelation concerning sexuality. This heritage also includes all the misuses of history to which our fears and neglect have led. Our religious tradition is both holy and wounded—and some of its wounds are self-inflicted. The Christian understanding of sex is both grace-filled and desperately in need of purification. Our religious history includes God's gifts and our malpractice. The task today is, as it has always been, to discern amid this marvelous and conflicted history the revelation that still excites us to faithful and generous love.

A second source in our reflection is the culture in which we live. Living in the United States at the beginning of the twenty-first century influences our perception of sexuality. Our religious heritage is complex and ambiguous; so too is our cultural inheritance. Pornography, consumerism, and popular entertainment affect our understandings of sex and our judgments about fidelity and commitment. But culture also makes other, more valuable, contributions to our appreciation of sexuality. In this book we draw on information available in psychological research and therapeutic practice. This information concerns a range of issues that influence mature sexuality. We give particular attention to the growing body of research and theory that takes up the thorny issues of gender—similarities and differences between women and men.

A third important source in this reflection is the lived experience of Christians today—the wisdom of the body. A dialogue between theology and the social sciences remains sterile unless it is joined by the testimony of mature Christians in the variety of lifestyles that constitute the community of faith. A traditional theological category for this wisdom of the community is *the sense of the faithful.* This ancient but largely forgotten metaphor points to a *sense* or *intuition* that belongs to the body of believers. The metaphor comes close to our image of visceral wisdom. A century ago John Cardinal Newman described this sense of faith as "a sort of instinct . . . deep in the bosom of the mystical body." Not yet articulated in a clear statement of doctrine, this knowledge is more a sensual sureness, rooted in the body's mature belief. A maturing Christian community, then, can possess a "sense" or instinct of what Christian faith requires. Included in this larger sense of the faithful are the believing community's understandings of sex, pleasure, commitment, fidelity, and fruitful love.

In the Second Vatican Council the church returned with some enthusiasm to this metaphor of the sense of the faithful. The Constitution on the Church, *Lumen Gentium,* for example, states that this active intuition "clings without fail to the faith once delivered to the saints, penetrates it more deeply by accurate insights and applies it more thoroughly to life." In the 1980 synod on Christian marriage, a number of participating bishops appealed to this practical wisdom that, abiding among married Christians whose instincts about married sexuality have been tested and refined over decades of faithful love, can teach the church—especially its unmarried leaders.

In both the thought of Cardinal Newman and the documents of Vatican II, this instinct of faith is understood to be more than simply a passive reflection of what is currently expressed in formal religious teaching. Newman believed that the community of faith must sometimes safeguard aspects of genuine belief that are being overlooked or neglected by religious officials. This may be especially true in sexual matters.

For centuries the church's official teaching portrayed marriage as "a remedy for concupiscence." This understanding, crafted by Augustine at the end of the fourth century, argues that marriage exists as a haven for the lustful. If one must use others for personal sexual pleasure (the definition of concupiscence), at least do so in marriage. Then the evil of promiscuity will not be added to that of lust, and responsibility can be taken for children—the fruit of one's passion. This definition of marriage became part of church law and shaped Catholic teaching about marriage for almost sixteen hundred years. Finally, the reformulation of church law in 1983 officially dropped this demeaning definition of marriage.

But throughout these sixteen hundred years, deep in the body Christian, another religious conviction prevailed. Many married Catholics recognized a very different truth about marriage. From their experience they knew that sexual arousal is about more than lust, that sexual delight is not always selfish. In a wisdom often unspoken, these couples came to know and cherish the links between pleasure and generous love. The sexual relationship they shared made life richer and more spiritually significant.

This wisdom of married Catholics survived in private. Seldom did they question or directly challenge the "official position" of the church. If church teaching on some sexual question contradicted their experience, then they had to be wrong or, at least, they had to keep quiet about their differences. So, many lay Christians held on to their conscientious judgments and remained mute. But their public silence deprived the Christian community of important resources of faith. Instead of lively debate the Christian community often settled for dead formulas for sexual conduct.

But today the body speaks. Lay Christians seem more confident and determined to share their vision of sexuality. Dick Westley encourages the Christian community to break its silence:

> It is time for sexually active believers to proclaim in the Lord's name, and without fear, what they have learned in bed, confident that it is, when communally funded, as authoritative as any episcopal letter or papal encyclical.

"Communally funded" means our experience as it is heard and tested in the Christian community. This is the objective of this book: to draw out and make public the sense of the faithful about Christians and their sexuality.

Three Options Today

When we face the confusing relationship of sexuality and Christianity, we may be drawn to respond in one of three ways. We may choose to interpret Christian tradition as a unified and absolute revelation. To do this we need to ignore or deny the seamier side of our religious history. In an effort to remain faithful to the church in a time of enormous transition, some of us may feel the need to affirm the tradition as it now stands, arguing for its unchanging stability, clarity, and rightness.

Another way to respond is simply to reject the tradition. A body of thought that contains so many negative attitudes toward sexuality, a history of pastoral practice that has offered so much harmful counsel, an institutional system that is punitive toward so many of its members—women, those who are divorced and remarried, persons who are homosexual—must be rejected, even denounced! Many persons, wounded by biases they feel they have learned from the church, now judge it to be bankrupt. The murky heritage of Christian belief and behavior around sex offers them no enduring values.

Others respond by acknowledging this complex religious tradition as both *mixed* and *mine*. Since Vatican II many Catholics have struggled with the institutional church and arrived at a deeper realization that they *are* Catholics—for better and for worse. The Catholic faith is our heritage and home. It is not a home that we choose to leave like angry children, but a home where we belong and for which we must care. We begin to recognize that the church, in its history and practice, is not simply the "unblemished spouse of Christ" or the "perfect society." Incomplete and wounded, it is very much like ourselves. The marvel of Christ's promise—"to be with you all days, even until the end of the world"—is that it is *this* church, this flawed, often shortsighted and sometimes arrogant group—ourselves—with whom God has promised to stay.

As we are stripped of a childish fantasy of a perfect and sinless church, we find that the conviction "we are the church" takes on a new and more powerful meaning. The reality of the church fits better with who we know ourselves to be. We can experience this as an invitation to a new level of participation in our religious faith. This third response can lead us to a more personal investment in our lovely but scarred heritage. We are called to help heal Christian prejudices against the body. And we are invited to recover the tradition's deepest convictions about the goodness of sexuality and the fruitfulness of love. In a lively dialogue among the Christian faith, our culture, and our personal experience we will be able to develop a spirituality of sexuality that is genuinely Christian, contemporary, and practical.

REFLECTIVE EXERCISE

We invite you, the reader, to participate in this reflection on the wisdom of the body Christian. At the end of each chapter we include a reflective exercise. The first goal of these exercises is self-exploration—to come to a clearer and more confident awareness of your own convictions on a particular issue or theme. Beyond that, our hope is that these exercises may be part of a larger effort to give voice to the wisdom of the body. The exercises are designed so that they may be used alone, but their value is often greatly enhanced by sharing with a friend or in a faith-sharing community or other small group setting. In these communal settings we may begin to see the links between the personal journey of faith and the emerging sense of the faithful.

In a time of quiet, recall the many images and convictions about sexuality that have come to you from the Christian tradition. These may be passages from scripture, memories of prayer or preaching, the attitudes of religious people. Take time to let the memories return.

After a while, choose one of these memories that speaks to you positively about sexuality. Spend time with it. What is the central conviction about sexuality that this religious memory holds for you? What are the feelings that accompany this memory?

Then turn to a memory or an image that is more negative in its view of sexuality. What information comes to you here about sexuality? What feelings return with this image?

Finally, think of your life today. Which of these religious convictions about sexuality has more influence on you now? Why do you think this is so?

ADDITIONAL RESOURCES

At the end of each chapter we will also provide information about references we use in the text as well as other resources on the chapter's themes and topics. A complete listing for each reference will be found in the Bibliography.

During the 1990s the Catholic bishops of the United States wrote three important pastoral letters related to sexuality: "Human Sexuality: A Catholic Perspective for Education and Lifelong Learning" (1991), "Follow the Way of Love: A Pastoral Message to Families" (1993), and "Always Our Children: A Pastoral Message to Parents of Homosexual Children and Suggestions for Pastoral Ministers" (1998).

In *Sex, Gender and Christian Ethics,* Lisa Sowle Cahill draws on contemporary scriptural research, Catholic moral tradition, feminist theological perspectives, and the findings of psychology for her discussion of the shape of Christian sexuality. Eugene Kennedy has long served the Christian community through his courageous and careful reflection on matters sexual and more; in *The Unhealed Wound* he examines the pastoral and psychological implications of the tradition's ambivalence about sex. Dick Westley offers his insightful reflections on sexuality in *Morality and Its Beyond* and *A Theology of Presence.* Patricia Martens Miller provides a sensitive practical guide to assist parents and teachers in *Sex Is* Not *a Four-Letter Word: Talking Sex with Your Children Made Easier.*

The document of the Second Vatican Council reinstating the sense of the faithful as an element in theological process is "The Constitution on the Church," *Lumen Gentium* (see §12). Cardinal Newman's analysis of the sense of the faithful appears in *On Consulting the Faithful in Matters of Doctrine.* We have explored the contemporary potential of this religious dynamic in Chapter 12 of our book *Community of Faith* and in Chapter 5 of *Seasons of Strength: New Visions of Adult Christian Maturing.*

2

The Good News about Sex

> Let him kiss me with the kisses of his mouth.
> Your love is more delightful than wine . . .
> I shall praise your love above wine;
> How good it is to love you.
> (Song of Songs 1:2, 4)

THE GOOD NEWS ABOUT SEX IS THAT SEX IS GOOD. The Catholic community's discussion of sex starts with this conviction, deeply rooted in the religious heritage we share as Jews and Christians. Part of the gift of creation, sexuality is good. In the community of faith today we eagerly affirm this ancient belief, true to our own experience as well.

Sex is good—a simple statement and yet one often disputed. Some see sex as evil, a source of shame to be avoided by those pursuing holiness. Others regard sex as an unpleasant, if necessary, part of the uneasy union of body and soul. Only in the institution of marriage can we cloak and control this embarrassing passion.

These negative evaluations of sex represent more than past history. Sex lies at the heart of the most vexing social problems of our own day: rape, incest, pornography, teenage pregnancy, abortion, AIDS. Sex perplexes our personal lives as well. We find ourselves both excited and confused by our bodies, with their desires and hesitancies. Some of our best moments in life—and some of our worst—involve sex. Our creativity finds expression in sex, as does our destructiveness. Genital arousal turns us outward in love and care; it can also turn us inward in self-absorption. In the face of this ambiguous evidence, the Christian conviction that "sex is good" comes as especially good news.

Christians believe that sex is good because our bodies are blessed and holy. "Your body is the temple of the Holy Spirit," St. Paul wrote to his friends in Corinth. God inhabits our bodies; the Creator delights to be present in this fleshly dwelling. But this conviction, at the heart of Christianity, remains incredible even to many Christians. The doctrine of the Trinity or the resurrection or the last judgment—these can be accepted on faith. But that God delights to dwell in *this* body—with its erections or menstruations or aching loneliness? Impossible! The contrary evidence seems too compelling: we use physical strength to strike out in violence; we misuse sex to abuse others and degrade ourselves. Too frequently our bodies are instruments of disorder, co-conspirators in our worst behavior.

Despite this negative experience, the Christian conviction stands: The body is holy; sex is good; God dwells here. The Incarnation, the reality at the very core of Christian history, reinforces this optimism. Being Hispanic may help one to recognize the word "flesh" (*carne*) in this abstract theological term. The Fourth Gospel tells us that "the Word was made flesh" (John 1:14). This is strong language. God becomes not a human being nor a moral agent nor a thinking person but *flesh*. God enters into a life like ours—physical, sexual, emotional. The Incarnation is good news for the flesh.

Sex Is Good

> How beautiful you are, my love,
> How beautiful you are!
> Your eyes, behind your veil, are doves . . .
>
> Your lips are a scarlet thread
> And your words enchanting . . .
> Your two breasts are two fawns . . .
> You are wholly beautiful, my love,
> And without blemish.
>   (Song of Songs 4:1, 3, 5, 7)

The Song of Songs, a lyrical poem about two lovers, helps us in the struggle to embrace the inherent goodness of sex. Neither a historical narrative nor a catalogue of laws, this brief text seems out of place in the Bible. To the surprise and even shock of many, the poem celebrates erotic love. In describing the arousal and passion of these lovers, the poem moves from explicit description to suggestive metaphor ("Let my beloved come into his garden; / Let him taste its rarest fruits" [4:16]).

This poetry has scandalized both Jews and Christians. What is this sexually provocative story doing in our sacred scripture? Because this book was originally ascribed to King Solomon, no one dared remove it from the canon. But how to explain or blunt its erotic message? Two historical efforts to "save" this text stand out. One method of interpretation viewed the poem as a dialogue between a bride and her bridegroom. Seeing these lovers as married makes their passion more legitimate. A second method of interpretation, the favorite for more than two thousand years, regarded the entire book as an allegory about the love between God and the human soul. Thus a poem about human, "profane love" was transformed into a story of pure (that is, nonsexual) devotion.

Recently scripture scholars have returned to the poem's most obvious meaning: the celebration of the goodness of sensual love. In this interpretation, the ancient poem can symbolize God's passionate love for us only because erotic love is itself good and holy. Christian morality has, of course, most often made sexuality's goodness dependent on fertility: making love is acceptable when a married couple intend to have a child. But this poem—part of Christian revelation—does not yet speak of children. Instead it lingers, with delight, on the essential goodness of sexual desire. In his commentary in *The Jerome Biblical Commentary,* Roland Murphy notes this special focus: "The course of events does not appear to be leading anywhere; the lover and beloved are simply enjoying each other's presence and affection."

The revelation here challenges Christians to reaffirm the goodness of sex. The poem itself concludes with a powerful assertion of the link between human passion and the flame of God's creation:

> For love is strong as death,
> Passion relentless as hell.
> The flash of it is a flash of fire,
> A flame of Yahweh's own self.
> (Song of Songs 8:6)

In returning to the original meaning of this poem, these scholars reinforce the wisdom of the body Christian. More and more members of the community of faith—lay people, pastoral ministers, theologians—urge the church toward a more wholehearted recognition that sex is good. These efforts are beginning to bear fruit. In preaching and pastoral counseling, in religious education programs and spiritual retreats, the good news about sex is becoming a lively part of Christian formation.

What is the truth that we, the Christian body, find in our sexual experience? We discover, first, the blessing of sexual arousal. This stirring in our bodies is one of the roots of our creativity; it draws us to others; it ignites the attraction that sustains the fruitful commitments of life—in friendship, in marriage, in devoted love. Second, we recognize that sexual love has more to do with fruitfulness than with fertility. Sex is, with its unexpected awakenings and unearned delights, an echo of creation. Third, we realize that in the touches and strokes of sexual sharing we are revealed to ourselves; we are brought to see a loveliness that we had been incapable of imagining on our own. And finally, we know that in our sexual lives we often find spiritual healing. Our physical embraces soothe old wounds and make forgiveness tangible. In the intimacy we share with a sexual partner, the reality of God's goodness and forgiveness finally becomes more than rhetoric. As lovers, we give thanks for this grace.

As Americans, we live in a society that complicates our attempts to tell the truth about sex. Even as we proclaim that sex is good, we know that it is not the only good. Sex participates in a community of human goods, an arena that includes generosity and justice and sacrifice. In adolescence, sex looms large; it excites and even threatens us as nothing else can. Maturing into adult life, we gradually befriend sex—we learn to appreciate its power, to savor its delights, to see through some of its illusions. We make decisions that integrate sexual activity into our lives in ways that are consistent with our deepest values.

Cultural forces can stunt this integration. America's fascination with sex, for example, coaxes all of us to linger too long in adolescence. Our society exalts sex as the peak experience and primary focus of life. The industry of pornography feeds this fantasy, but it thrives in more "respectable" forms as well—in advertising, in the media, in tabloid journalism. This national preoccupation takes sex out of context, separating pleasure from the accompanying dynamics of mutuality, responsibility, and commitment.

As Christians, we put sex in context by turning to the witness of Jesus in the Gospels. A first fact that impresses the reader is the relative absence of talk about sex. The Gospels reveal a life that is overwhelmingly concerned with change and healing. Jesus heals the sick and the possessed; he invites sinners to change their lives; he urges others to leave all and follow him in a different way of life. Personal change, conversion, and a life lived with and for others—these, rather than a set of specific instructions about moral behavior, form the core of Jesus' message.

As recorded in the Gospels, Jesus' mission did not include marriage. Christians have seen this as a sign of his radical commitment to the service of God. In his life and lifestyle Jesus speaks to us of the relative unimportance of everything beyond love and justice and the healing that these virtues can effect. Good and holy as it is, sex is not the most important aspect of life. Sex is a significant part of life and, for most of us, a central dynamic in both maturity and spirituality. But, Jesus' life witnesses, we are sexual and more. The Gospels thus invite us to take sex both more and less seriously than otherwise we might.

The body of Christ knows that sex is good, but that it is not ultimate. Sex is not the meaning of life. Sexual pleasure will not bear the weight of a life focused primarily on its pursuit. The life of Jesus challenges us all, married and unmarried, to a more than genital love, a larger than biological family, a fruitfulness that goes beyond biological fecundity. Some of us build lives of deep intimacy that do not include genital sharing. All of us learn the lessons of love that come only in seasons of abstinence—the death of a partner, the end of a friendship, the loss of consolation in prayer. In the midst of the challenges and invitations that surround our sexual lives, we proclaim our basic conviction: *sex is good.*

> In his longed-for shade I am seated
> And his fruit is sweet to my taste.
> He has taken me to his banquet hall,
> And the banner he raises over me is love.
>
> (Song of Songs 2:3–4)

Sex Is Mysterious

Over the past hundred years, medical research has expanded the understanding of human reproduction. This explosion of knowledge has produced effective new procedures for treating a range of problems: sexual dysfunction, infertility, at-risk pregnancies, birth defects.

It has also generated a host of complex ethical and legal questions related to reproduction—issues from birth control and abortion to in-vitro fertilization and surrogate parenting. During this same time, social scientists have been studying patterns of sexual behavior. These investigators—Sigmund Freud at the turn of the century, Alfred Kinsey and his associates in the 1940s and '50s, William Masters and Elizabeth Johnson more recently, to cite only a few—have described the actual sexual behavior of women and men. Here again, the findings have been significant, inviting a reexamination of many previously accepted assumptions—about masturbation, homosexuality, sexual behavior in marriage, and the physical responsiveness of women and of men.

But there remains so much we still do not understand. Those most involved in the study of sex are the first to acknowledge our continuing ignorance. Physiologically and psychologically, much about the human experience of sex remains unclear. Part of the mystery of sex is rooted here, in the limits of our current understanding.

But what we do know about sex is hardly less mysterious. For instance, sexual reproduction links the human species with the rest of the animal kingdom. But the arena of sex is one in which humans differ most from other animals. For most animals, sex is seasonal. For a brief period of time at a biologically determined stage of development males and females are capable of mating. Outside such a mating season most animals display no sexual activity. The attraction and union of women and men, by contrast, does not depend on a mating season. Sexual activity among humans is less controlled by biological cues.

In most animals, sexual activity is narrowly focused on reproduction. For example, among the primates closest to humans in evolutionary development—the great apes—the female is receptive to the male's sexual approach only during estrus, a recurring but relatively brief period of biological fertility. Among humans, in contrast, sexual interest is not limited to reproductive periods. A woman can experience sexual arousal throughout the menstrual cycle, not just during the limited phase when conception is possible. Both women and men remain interested in and capable of genital behavior long after their biological fertility has come to an end. This would seem to confirm that for the human species sex is about more than reproduction.

The links between pleasure and genital behavior deepen the mystery of human sex. In many animals, physical agitation marks sexual readiness, and sexual release reestablishes physiological calm. But there is little evidence that many species experience genital activity itself as pleasurable. For humans, sex and pleasure are intimately linked. And the links seem to go beyond the commonsense explanation that sexual pleasure is the decoy nature uses to draw otherwise reluctant humans (especially the male of the species) into the onerous responsibilities of parenthood. Consider, for example, the role of the female clitoris. When appropriately stimulated in lovemaking, the clitoris is a significant source of pleasure for most women. Yet biology identifies no reproductive purpose for this organ. Unlike the multipurpose male penis, the clitoris seems to function simply in the service of sexual delight. Even physiologically, human sexuality is about more than reproduction.

The mystery of sex includes the ambiguities of our own experience. Sex is a source of our greatest delights and of our most painful confusions. In sexual experience we can come to a profound awareness of our own goodness and worth. In sex we also come face to face with the inner conflicts and compulsions that drive us. Sexual sharing sometimes brings a communion so profound that it shatters the shield of our isolation. We can also use sex to punish ourselves, to control other people, to diminish joy.

Sex is mysterious in its meanings. Sex is almost always about something more or something else. One of Sigmund Freud's most influential (and most controversial) contributions has been to show that much apparently nonsexual behavior is sexually motivated. Therapists today remind us that the reverse is also true: factors that have little to do with sex motivate a good deal of sexual behavior—from flirting to masturbation to intercourse. Rape is an extreme example. This violent act finds roots in aggression and hostility more than in sexual passion.

Sex is symbolic. It escapes any simple definition. Consider the different answers that people give to the question of what sex means. Some people look at sex as recreational; they focus on pleasure, on sex as diversion and delight. Sex certainly does re-create us. But to view sex as primarily recreational leads to the moral stance of casual sex: among consenting adults, as long as no one is hurt, "anything goes." This partial view neglects the connections and consequences of our sexual actions; it fails to tell the whole truth about sex.

Other people appreciate sex as relational. Focusing on the quality of the relationship, they view sex as a gift to be exchanged between friends. This is true. But to view sex as simply relational leads to the moral stance of companionate sex. In this understanding, sex is appropriately shared in a relationship where there is genuine affection and concern for each other, even without expectations of continuity, exclusivity, or permanent commitment.

Many people regard sex as reproductive. Here the focus is biological, stressing sex as the means of human reproduction. Clearly this too is true. When reproduction is seen as the dominant truth about sex, the moral stance concentrates on the links between sex and marriage. Then sex is appropriate only within legally sanctioned marriage and only in the service of biological reproduction.

The body of Christ acknowledges the truth of each of these perspectives—and goes beyond. For Christians, sex is sacramental. This predominant truth is not so much antagonistic to these other perspectives as it is complementary. The recognition of sex as sacramental does not contradict the truth that sex is re-creative, relational, and reproductive. Rather it places these insights—each true, each partial—in a larger context of meaning.

Sex is sacramental. This is part of its mystery. St. Paul described the uniting of a man and woman in marital love as "a great mystery" (Ephesians 5:32). When this phrase in Ephesians was translated into Latin and then English, the "mystery" of marriage became the "sacrament" of marriage. For Paul marriage is a mystery in the same way that the Christian community as the body of Christ is a mystery. Sex is sacramental because it is suggestive, reminding us not only of the mutual commitment of this couple but of our link with our Creator. Our passionate unions resonate with that covenant of affection and fidelity that God has made with humankind. This ability of our sexual lives to hint at God's presence among us makes sexuality sacramental and holy.

In its fierce privacy and its unavoidable socialness, sexual life symbolizes the life of faith. The covenant between us and God, made in the deepest recesses of our heart, affects all our public behavior. The church has long cherished the image of marriage as a compelling metaphor of its own commitment and fidelity with God. Sex is mysterious because it is sacramental: it can remind us of God's passionate affection for us. For this reason, too, sex is very good.

Sex Makes Promises

"The last time we made love was sad, violent, filled with the awfulness of endings." This poignant sentence opens Sam Keen's account, in *The Passionate Life,* of an affair in which "good sex" gradually turns sour. Two persons had come together from very different lives, united more in flight than in pursuit.

> So we finally agreed to meet in exile, on the island of the flesh. When the heat was upon us, we came together, made love, had a meal together, and went our separate ways. We pretended the void between us was neutral space.

But the balm of sex did not work its reputed wonders. A mood of discontent interfered with delight; the relationship began to disintegrate. Having agreed that sex would make no promises, these lovers found that

> something in us did not respect our contract. Our agreement to sever sense from spirit violated our longing for the unconditional. The ghost of the bonds we would not acknowledge returned to haunt us, until we came to hate each other for all that was missing.

". . . for all that was missing . . ." Keen's moving lament recalls another conviction of the body Christian. Sex is not a neutral ingredient in our relationship; sex changes things. Sex generates more than passion; a sexual relationship arouses hopes and enkindles expectations. As sexual sharing continues, promises are made—sometimes explicitly, often in more subtle ways. Recreational sex is bankrupt not because it focuses on pleasure but because it does not keep its promises.

Sex makes promises. This is part of the wisdom of the body Christian. The problem with casual sex is that keeping sex casual is difficult. A couple may come together determined simply to have an enjoyable sexual relationship. "We like each other and want to give each other pleasure," they avow, "but with 'no strings attached.'" They agree on this limited arrangement, but the experience develops differently. Beyond their plans, even against their conscious ambitions, they confront the deeper issues of sexuality. They find that physical intimacy and psychological intimacy are connected. Sex play reveals more than their bodies; it often uncovers hidden hurts and fragile hopes. In their lovemaking, more than pleasure is aroused. Sex raises issues of dependence and commitment, even when these matters have been ruled out of bounds. Casual lovers come to admit: "We started out with modest expectations of one another. At first, we just depended on each other to be available when we had agreed—in a good mood, if possible! But our expectations started to expand; it's as though we couldn't help expecting more from each other. We began to look for deeper ways to share our lives with one another. We began to depend on one another for understanding and support, even more than for sex!"

Sex goes somewhere. That, in fact, is part of its fascination. Sexual intimacy has intellectual and emotional ramifications that extend beyond our immediate control. Sexual sharing can move us beyond ourselves; it can lead us deeper into our relationship. Sex and love are not the same thing. We learn, often from our mistakes, how risky and confusing the two can be. But if sex and love are not identical, they are closely related in human experience. At its best, sex is about making love. And love carries a future, for it brings with it both shared hopes and mutual obligations.

The word *lovemaking* reminds us that sex is about more than the experience of pleasure or the discharge of tension. Making love generates new life—sometimes in the generation of children, more often in nurturing the deepening bonds of mutual care.

Sexual love gives new life; this is part of the wisdom of the body of Christ. If love is to endure, it must be creative beyond itself. This is true of sexual love as much as of compassionate care. Sexual attraction often begins in a stage of mutual fascination. Enthralled with each other, the lovers find everything about the other person engrossing. Little beyond their absorption with one another seems worthy of attention. The world tolerates this attitude in lovers—at least for a while. We know this shared obsession represents an early phase of romance; but soon infatuation passes. The relationship may mature into a deeper love, or it may die from lack of any further substance. But in either case the charmed circle of sexual fascination will be breached. Soon the lovers will rejoin the rest of us—better, we trust, for the experience.

Sex points beyond itself. Sexual love, as it grows, moves beyond mutual absorption. We learn that being *for* one another does not require us to be indifferent to everyone else. Love enriches us, giving us more of what is best in each of us. We feel the impetus to move beyond ourselves, to share this blessing, to bring the power of our love to others.

Love that does not look beyond itself will die—Christian wisdom has long proclaimed this sometimes fleeting insight of our own experience. Moralists have sometimes expressed this truth in narrowly biological terms—that every genital act must be open to the conception of a child. Many Catholics today, especially married persons, find this statement of the connection between sex and generative love to be at odds with their own experience; it is too restrictive. Riveting attention on fertility makes of sex both too much and too little. This approach places too much emphasis on particular activities, but fails to recognize the broader contributions of sex to the full range of fruitful love. The Christian conviction remains: an essential connection exists between making love and giving life. But the wisdom of the body proclaims that this connection has more to do with fruitfulness than with fertility.

> On my bed at night I sought him
> Whom my heart loves.
> I sought but did not find him.
> So I will rise and go through the city,
>
> In the streets and the squares
> I will seek him whom my heart loves.
> (Song of Songs 3:1–2)

While sex can be fun, experience teaches that it is not to be treated lightly. Recently a friend recounted a conversation she had shared with her young adult daughter, Mimi, who had enjoyed a casual friendship with Dan for several years. During their senior year in college, the friendship between Mimi and Dan began to deepen. As their affection grew more passionate, sex became part of the relationship. "Sex is really confusing," Mimi confided to her mother. "Dan and I agree that marriage was not what we want now, with both of us just beginning graduate school. We love each other a lot and are still really good friends, but things are different since we started sleeping together. I'm not even sure I can say exactly what the difference is. Lovemaking is great, but there's a lot more tension between us. Dan and I talk about it sometimes. We've decided maybe it's just that sex complicates a relationship."

Sex complicates a relationship. Mimi and Dan are not alone in this realization. "Sex stirs longings in us that are not easily stilled," psychologist Lillian Rubin confirms. For most people, even in this age that recommends "cool sex," sexual sharing changes a relationship—sometimes for the better, sometimes for the worse, often both. The cultural norms of an earlier generation suggested that psychological intimacy precedes sexual intimacy. Many of us now in midlife grew up with the expectation that sexual sharing would come only after a couple knew each other well. In the relationships of many young adults today this expectation is reversed: sexual intimacy precedes psychological depth or even emotional closeness. The sense seems to be "if we are good together sexually, we may be willing to face the riskier challenge of sharing our lives." In whatever direction the couple moves—from psychological to physical intimacy, or vice versa—experience still confirms the conviction: sex changes a relationship.

Sexual sharing opens new questions—of trust and vulnerability, of belonging and commitment, of autonomy and interdependence. These issues arise even for couples who, like Dan and Mimi, have decided ahead of time that sex does not imply anything beyond here and now. While we may declare the bigger questions out of bounds, that simple declaration seldom succeeds. Questions of trust and commitment continue to arise. We find ourselves relying on each other more and more. Whatever our verbal agreements, our sexual embraces continue to promise more.

Sex is promising because it can hold us together in the midst of difficult changes. Early on, before we have found our rhythm of compromise and reconciliation, we can expect some rocky times. Often our sexual sharing soothes some of these confusions. Sex, of course, cannot of itself heal a troubled relationship. But it can remind us of the delight of our mutual love and can promise that we will come through these difficulties.

The promises of sexual love are real but fragile. Passion hints at a union between us that goes beyond the joining of our bodies. But passion comes and goes. Our lovemaking confirms that "we fit together well," luring us to link our lives in other ways. But to forge these links we must depend on more than the spontaneous delights of sex. The promises sex makes are not well kept in casual encounter. These promises need a home, a protected place in which to grow.

The body Christian knows that sex finds its home in commitment. Commitment gives passion a place to flower and be fruitful. For many people, the form that this commitment takes is marriage. As a legal contract, marriage is the sanctioned shape of enduring sexual commitment. As a religious covenant, marriage is a sign and source of God's love. The commitments of marriage—communion, fidelity, permanence—provide a framework that can protect and purify the promises of sexual love.

But the supportive framework of marriage is not available to all. Today many homosexual couples seek a public commitment to affirm and protect the promises that their love generates. Until recently, both cultural norms and religious ethics have denied the potential of such sexual intimacy. Convinced that these unions are unpromising, societies act in ways that contribute to keeping these encounters casual and uncommitted. While social and religious pressures against homosexuality do not prevent sexual sharing, they can undermine hopes of fidelity and duration. These social attitudes ignore the lives of lesbian and gay couples who *do* realize the promises of healthy interdependence and enduring commitment. These lives, if we would but welcome their testimony, have much to teach us about the promise of human love.

Marriage is not part of every life, and the commitments of marriage are not the only context that supports the promise of love. In the community of faith today, growing numbers of adults are not married—some have never married, others are divorced or widowed. All of us—single or married, gay or straight, celibate or sexually active—look to Jesus Christ as the paradoxical instructor in the good news about sex. The Gospels give us no information about Jesus' sexual life, content with the assurance that he is "like to us in all ways except sin." This unmarried and childless person shows us many ways to love. And from his life we learn the criteria of Christian love: mutual respect rather than coercion or selfishness; the deepening of commitment and fidelity; the healing of injuries; the quickening of courage.

The Word made Flesh is good news for the body. The revelation of God that has been given in Jesus Christ has significance for our sexual lives. From its outset Christianity has struggled, not always successfully, to express this good news in ways that illumine, purify, and liberate love. This effort continues today, as the community of faith gives voice to its experience. Married couples acknowledge the range of pleasures that makes their life together fruitful. Single adults speak out concerning the place of sexuality in their lives. Mature Christians who are lesbian or bisexual or gay tell the church—sometimes hesitantly, sometimes courageously—how sexuality and spirituality are part of their own experience. As Christians learn to listen well to one another we recognize that, in our sexuality as in so much else, we are more alike than we are different. Across our different lifestyles, we share similar concerns as we struggle to fashion faithful and generous ways to express our love. In these diverse experiences our shared conviction is confirmed—*sex is good.*

REFLECTIVE EXERCISE

Draw on your own experience of the good news about sex. In a prayerful mood, spend time with the convictions in this chapter.

Sex is good.

In what ways do you know sex to be good? How does your own experience confirm this conviction?

Where does your experience lead you to challenge or question this optimistic stance toward sex?

Where in Christian life today do you find this appreciation of sex most authentically presented?

Sex is mysterious.

Consider the ways in which the mystery of sex is real for you. How is sex surprising? How is sex confusing? How is sex profound?

What practical meaning is there, in your own experience, to the phrase "sex is sacramental"?

Sex makes promises.

Recall your own life or the experiences of others you know well. What are the promises that sex makes—the hopes and expectations that accompany sexual sharing?

In your own awareness, what are the connections between sex and commitment? Between sex and fidelity? Between sex and fruitfulness?

ADDITIONAL RESOURCES

In *The Jerome Biblical Commentary,* Roland Murphy offers a brief overview of current scholarship concerning Song of Songs. Ariel Bloch and Chana Bloch provide a beautiful volume, with English and Hebrew text on facing pages, in their edition of *The Song of Songs.* Raymond Collins traces the connections between discipleship and sexuality in the texts of the New Testament in *Sexual Ethics and the New Testament.*

Elizabeth Dryer discusses sexual love as a building block for spirituality in *Earth Crammed with Heaven: A Spirituality of Everyday Life.* In *The Holy Longing* Ronald Rolheiser sets out the gracious parameters of an authentically Christian spirituality of sexuality. Joan Timmerman explores the positive convictions that are part of the Christian tradition in *Sexuality and Spiritual Growth.* In *Extravagant Affections,* Susan Ross offers a feminist sacramental theology that takes seriously the implications of sexuality and embodiment.

Sam Keen explores the experience of love in *The Passionate Life.* In *The Soul of Sex,* Thomas Moore looks into the psychological and spiritual implications of our sexual humanity. In *Sex: The Catholic Experience,* Andrew Greeley provides an insightful analysis of results from a national study. For an examination of the findings of comprehensive research on sexual practice in the United States, see *Sex, Love and Health in America: Private Choices and Public Policy,* edited by Edward Laumann and Robert Michael, and *Sexuality in America: Understanding Our Sexual Values and Behavior,* edited by Patricia Koch and David Weis.

3

Eros and Sexuality

THE BODY GIVES GIFTS TO THE SPIRIT. The lazy contentment of a summer day, an invigorating walk along the seashore, the warmth of a loving embrace, the pleasures of a meal shared with friends—these are benefits of our bodyliness. In our bodies we are stirred by beauty and moved by emotion. Our bodies want to be touched—held in affection, caressed by a lover, soothed by a comforting hand. The body delights in making contact.

Eros is the traditional name given to the body's desire and delight. In early Greek mythology Eros was the vital force active in every area of life. In contemporary usage, however, *eros* has a considerably narrower meaning. The closest we get to *eros* is *erotic*, a word that suggests to many people a perverse preoccupation with sex. The erotic has vaguely pornographic connotations, calling up images of seedy adult bookstores and sleazy massage parlors.

Many theologians and psychologists today are appealing to the broader classical meaning of eros as the sensual face of love. Rooted in our bodies, our sensuality encompasses more than sex. Eros is our passionate drive for life and growth. This meaning of erotic experience includes much more than genital arousal. Eros moves in all our longings to make contact, to be—quite literally—*in touch*. Arousal and affection, passion and response, intimacy and appreciation—these are all part of eros. In erotic experience we first feel the connections between presence and pleasure, between longing and new life.

The Importance of Touch

Silence shrouds the scene. Visitors move slowly along the wall of names. On this rainy day at the Vietnam War Memorial, no one is in a rush. Coming to the name he had been searching for, a man squints at the letters etched in marble. Then his hand reaches up to touch the imprint. Fingers edge slowly along the marks, spelling the name one more time.

Others repeat this poignant exercise of touching. Their fingers make contact with cold, wet stone. But watching their faces and tears, any observer can see they are touching much more than this wall. At this secular liturgy, repeated a hundred times daily, human touch performs its magic. Contact with mere stone is able to release memories and emotion. Pain and anger are summoned from some hidden spot; griefs are mourned again in a touch that both salutes and says good-bye.

Touch is a good example of the breadth and complexity of eros. In infancy, if we are fortunate, our parents hold and stroke and caress us. They wrap us in protective embraces that our memories still savor. Nursing, we taste the nourishing pleasures of touch. Soon our hands begin to explore the wonderful terrain of our own bodies—until we are instructed in the limits of this delight.

As children we experience the feel of cold sheets as we jump into bed on a winter night, the comforting texture of a familiar sweater, the delight of burying our face in a pet's luxurious hairy coat. But our memories of childhood may also include touch as a vehicle of punishment. Spankings and slaps or more violent reminders teach us that contact is not just about pleasure. Still, our memories, unless they are so injured that they flee into amnesia, carry a rich history of our sensual contact with life.

In early adolescence the power of touch explodes in the experience of puberty. Suddenly our bodies become alert and eager for touch. Here, too, we confront the complexity of pleasure: our delight does not always guarantee someone else's pleasure; passion is not always mutual; touch can injure and humiliate as well as comfort.

Because we are so easily aroused by touch in adolescence, we may equate every touch with genital arousal. Dressing and bathing carry extra meaning; the casual touch of a friend excites us. Frightened by the links between touch and sexuality, we may start to avoid every kind of contact. In an effort to control the forbidden pleasures of touch, we keep to ourselves.

In time we may come to be "out of touch"—with friends, our own bodies, any tactile pleasure. We learn to abstain from reassuring hugs, relaxing back rubs, a friendly arm around the shoulder—touches that have echoes of genital arousal. We may conclude that whenever another person touches us, the contact and its pleasure have but one, genital meaning. This restricts the possibilities for intimacy in our life.

Maturing as sensual persons we learn that the pleasures of touch are many and different—not every touch is a genital signal; not every pleasurable contact is meant to initiate sexual sharing. In truth, the sensual can enrich our lives well beyond the pleasure of genital arousal. But often we need to recover this rich resource. Revisiting the Gospel of Mark and observing Jesus touching others may help us appreciate anew our own sensuality. In Mark's Gospel we meet a very human Jesus, frequently in physical contact with other people. At dinner one evening a woman approaches and anoints Jesus' head with an expensive, fragrant oil. This sensual action startles and offends his companions. To deal with their discomfort about this unseemly intimacy, they argue about extravagance and waste. But Jesus responds, "Leave her alone!" He likes to be touched this way.

Throughout the good news recounted by Mark, those who are ill seek Jesus out. When they find him, Jesus often touches them in a way that changes their life. And Jesus seems to *need to touch them*. In the Gospel account of his healing a blind man, Jesus mixes some dirt with his own spit and presses the mud into the person's eyes; gradually the man regains his sight. In another story Jesus praises the simplicity of a group of children. "Then he put his arms around them, laid his hands on them and gave them his blessing" (Mark 10:16).

In one of the most compelling narratives of Jesus' contact with others, an ill woman approaches him with the conviction, "If I can touch even his clothes, I will be well again" (Mark 5:28). Jesus comes to a stop, aware that he has been touched in some special way. He asks who has touched him, and his friends are surprised since they are jostling their way through a thick crowd. But Jesus tells them that he felt power going out of him. Like the hands on the war memorial wall, human touch made something happen. Touch has this mysterious power to heal—if we know how to recognize its sensual force.

Theologian Tom Driver gives us a wonderful example of touch as an element of healing. Driver describes how he awoke one summer morning after a late night of long conversations. Fatigued and foggy at that quiet morning hour, he felt both a complaint and a request arising from his body:

> Tired limbs and untoned muscle spoke to him. "Wash us," they said. There was a chorus of complaint in his body. "Take care of me. Treat me with love."

In this moment of leisure, his body made its plea for attention. It begged for sensual contact and healing. During a long and leisurely bath, Driver came in touch again with parts of his body that he had too long neglected. "He remembered that in forty-eight years and in spite of a deeply sensual nature he had never quite made peace with his body." In the course of this sensual meditation, Driver recognized that his body—in its stiffness—harbored some unforgiven hurts. Driver's long meditation brings the Christian theme of reconciliation to bear on our own bodyliness. Our bodies long for the wholeness and salvation that our religious rhetoric preaches. They carry ancient memories of guilt and shame that need healing; they do not want so much to be forgiven as to be loved. Here as in the Gospel, the needed healing can be communicated in the sensual experience of touch.

The Language of Sexuality

This man caressing his body in a bath provides a good example of the ambiguity of eros. Many of us have found only a genital meaning in sensual exploration. Driver reminds us that our bodies give us more than the gift of genital delight. But as we recognize the wider scope of sensuality, we are brought to the question of interpretation. We learn to assign certain meanings to our body's stirrings. These interpretations take us into the realm of sexuality. Sexuality expresses our attempts—as a people and as individual persons—to make sense of and manage erotic life. Sexuality, then, is what we make of sex. We begin our consideration of sexuality with a look at vocabulary.

Sex, sexuality, intimacy—in ordinary speech these words seem interchangeable. But even when we use the terms as synonyms, we do not consider them to be equally respectable. The word *sex* sometimes seems too blunt to be used in polite company. The word *sexuality* is more acceptable, for the added syllables somehow soften the impact. But most preferable is the term *intimacy*—a genteel code word to cover any necessary or unavoidable references to genital activity.

But if these three words are used interchangeably in casual speech, they are recognized as different by most careful observers. Sex, sexuality, intimacy—each refers to a particular realm of adult experience. These experiences are related and often overlap, but they are not the same. We can picture their relationship in three concentric circles. In this image, the smallest circle is the realm of sex. Sexuality, the next larger circle, holds within it the experience of sex but includes more. The largest circle, intimacy, takes in the realms of sex and sexuality but goes beyond to include other kinds of closeness. We will examine intimacy in Chapter 4; here we want to explore differences between sex and sexuality.

The Realm of Sex

The word *sex* carries two related meanings. First, sex refers to the reproductive organs. It points to the biological systems of the adult male and female that are involved in human reproduction and in the experience of genital pleasure. In this meaning, sex is rooted in the x and y chromosomes of genetic inheritance and depends on pre- and postnatal hormonal activity for proper development. Here sex concerns the biological aspect of *who we are.*

The word *sex* is also used to refer to genital behavior. Here sex is about *what we do.* Included here are all those activities that are part of genital arousal and that can lead to orgasm—from sexual feelings and fantasies to self-stimulation, love play, and intercourse.

The Scope of Sexuality

The word *sexuality* ushers us into a more complex reality. Our sexuality includes the realm of sex—that is, our reproductive organs and our genital behavior—but encompasses much more of who we are. What our body means to us, how we understand our self as a woman or as a man, the ways we feel comfortable in expressing affection—these are part of our sexuality.

Theologian James Nelson reminds us that sexuality "involves much more than what we *do* with our genitals." The more has to do with meaning. Sexuality moves us beyond biology toward the social expectations and cultural ideals that influence us. Sexuality reflects the human effort—in language, in art, in moral reflection—to give meaning to sex. In this broadest sense, sexuality is how we make sex significant.

Our society teaches us what sex signifies: romance and "sexiness" are products of culture, not of biology. Our Christian heritage, too, assigns meaning and value to sexual behavior: chastity and celibacy, for example, reflect religious interpretations of sex. Our culture and religious faith guide us, for better and for worse, in making sense of sex.

Our sexuality is rooted in a particular consciousness we have about ourselves. This self-understanding comes in part from our own experience, but it is influenced by the messages we receive from our family, our school, and our church, and from the values and biases of our culture. Our parents' easy display of their affection for one another teaches us to be comfortable with physical closeness. A high school counselor's reassurance as we struggle with masturbation helps us accept some of the confusions of the adolescent experience of sex. Hollywood's romanticized version of beauty leaves us self-conscious about our physical appearance and envious of others who come closer to the "ideal body." These awarenesses—these understandings of our self—are the building blocks of our sexuality.

Being Embodied

Three elements of this self-awareness are crucial. The first is a sense of embodiment—what having a body, being a "body-ed" self means. We use different images to express the relationship between self and body. Sometimes the experience is one of integration—body and self are one. Athletes experience this when they are able to perform complicated physical tasks with both ease and skill. This is part of the high that comes in sports, for player and spectator alike. In viewing the film *Chariots of Fire,* even the non-joggers among us could sense this integration as the champion runner declared: "When I run I feel God's pleasure." Something similar often occurs in lovemaking, when the barrier of separateness is momentarily transcended and lovers experience a communion that goes beyond the joining of bodies.

But our experiences of embodiment are not always so positive. At times—in illness, perhaps, or "the morning after the night before"—self and body seem disconnected, linked only in an uneasy truce. We may know periods of even greater antagonism, when an unwilling body cages our spirit or when the unruly demands of the flesh defy the soul. This was the agony that St. Paul experienced: "My body follows a different law that battles against the law which my reason dictates. . . . What a wretched man I am! Who will rescue me from this body doomed to death?" (Romans 7:23–24). Now our body seems to become the enemy.

These images of embodiment capture the changing sense of what being a body/self means. Some images may be fleeting: after breaking a leg, we experience our body as a cumbersome burden. But the cast is soon removed and we quickly feel strong and agile again. Other images linger, becoming part of the characteristic way we see our self—our body is clumsy or sickly or fat-and-ugly. These images of our embodiment become a significant part of our sexuality.

Being "Gendered"

A second aspect of our sexuality is gender—what being a woman or a man means. This awareness comes in part from our sex, that is, from the fact that our reproductive system is female or male. But our sense of our self as a man or a woman involves much more than a check of reproductive organs. Gender goes beyond biology to social expectations. If sex is about male and female, gender is about masculine and feminine. Gender says less about how we are equipped than about how we should act.

Each culture forms its own roles and rules of gender. By determining what is appropriate for women and for men, the social group establishes its working categories of feminine and masculine. These definitions may differ from culture to culture, but every society develops gender expectations. Our society's expectations about what is masculine and feminine play an important role in our growing sense of what being a woman or a man means.

Our awareness that we are a woman (or a man) is central to our sexuality. Initially we come to this sense through the messages we receive from others, especially from our parents. From them we learn that "since you are a girl, you shouldn't fight back" or that "our little girl can be anything she wants to be." As we participate in school and church and neighborhood, we learn broader expectations of femininity—what is necessary to be accepted as a girl/woman. In our community and in the media, we find role models who show us what being a woman means. We discover both the benefits and the burdens of our gender.

Through this process of gender identification, we come to hold ourselves accountable to the norms of femininity that prevail in the group that is important to us. But the match is seldom perfect. As we compare our self to the culture's image of a woman, we find both similarities and differences. Critical to our sexuality is what we do about the differences.

A cultural image of either masculinity or femininity is always close to a stereotype, because this image disregards the remarkable range of individual differences. Every woman, for example, has feelings and talents and hopes that do not fit the culture's description of what a woman is or should be. The parts of themselves that do not fit, that are not "feminine," embarrass many women. We may be more assertive than a "good woman," or too tall and too athletic to be really "feminine," or "unnaturally" more interested in living out a dream of personal accomplishment than in having children. Men who confront the "unmasculine" parts of themselves—tenderness or nurturance or the desire to be held—experience a similar dichotomy between what they are and how their culture defines them.

Mature sexuality challenges us to come gradually to greater confidence and comfort with the way that we are women (or men). In doing this we acknowledge the ways that our experience fits the social norm, and we accept the parts of our self that contradict the culture's expectations. For both men and women, maturity also urges us to question cultural definitions and social norms of gender that distort our common humanity.

Gender differences influence our stance toward relationships as well as our self-awareness. We will explore these differences more fully in Chapter 9.

Expressing Affection

A third critical part of our sexuality concerns the movement of our affections, the feelings that we have toward persons of the same and of the opposite sex. Here again culture is critical, telling us what are appropriate feelings to have toward women and toward men. In this way the culture defines the categories of heterosexual and homosexual experience. Each of us, then, must come to terms with the movements of our own affectional life. As men, for example, we learn that U.S. culture permits us to be sexually attracted to women and to show them physical affection. We also learn that the display of physical affection between men is discouraged. Our culture views with suspicion a man who is emotionally drawn toward other men. With this cultural backdrop, each of us has to sort out and accept our own experiences of physical and emotional attraction.

Most of us, both women and men, find that our own feelings do not fit neatly into the culture's narrowest definitions of acceptable heterosexuality. We are drawn, to different degrees and with different intensity, toward both men and women. Some of us find that our strongest emotional orientation is toward persons of the same sex. This level of self-awareness—the ways we are moved emotionally by women and by men, the sense we have of our self as primarily gay, lesbian, bisexual, or heterosexual—is part of our sexuality.

Sexuality and the Sensual

Taking us beyond sexual activity, sexuality includes a sense of embodiment, an awareness of gender, the movements of affection. This last aspect reminds us of the intimate links between sexuality and our emotional life. Emotions are the feelings that *move* us. Anger stirs us; compassion arouses us; sorrow and guilt cast us down. Our emotions, like our sexuality, are rooted in bodily arousal. This does not mean that our emotional experiences are "really" genital, but that our ability to respond—in anger or sympathy or delight—is an aspect of our sexuality.

Our life constricts when we respond to others only in physical arousal and when we express closeness only in genital ways. Attraction and responsiveness remain aspects of sexuality even when they have little to do with genital sex. To be attracted by another's goodness, to be drawn to beauty in nature, to be moved by music and art—these emotional responses often stir us physically and enrich our lives.

Evidence from personal lives and from psychological research indicates that these emotional responses are part of the broader experience of sexuality. Hostility toward our body and fear of our emotions are often linked. If we are confused about our masculinity, we may find that reaching out to other people in genuine friendship is difficult. If we are afraid of the ways in which our affections are stirred, we may retreat into a stance of no response at all. Soon the experiences of joy and beauty become as alien to us as the unwanted sexual stimulation.

The sensual is another name for the many ways that we are bodily moved, excited, and refreshed. This is the broader meaning of eros and sexuality. Let us listen to the impressive range of our sensual stirrings . . .

A long and exhausting week of work has finally ended, and I am driving home past a large lake. For once I notice what I usually ignore: the gentle lapping of the water. Attracted by this sight, I park my car and sit at the lakeside watching the waves rhythmically massage the shoreline. Soon they do the same to some hardened interior coastline. Something in me lets go its grip; my body begins to relax a bit. A very gentle but clear arousal is taking place within me. If I pay attention, I can feel the sensual delight. . . .

On a rainy Saturday afternoon I decide to listen to some music. The children are away. I turn off the telephone and settle down to this favorite relaxation. Before long the music insinuates itself into my body. Distraction and dissipation give way to a more peaceful mood. The music engenders a harmony, a feeling of being connected again with the universe (not with my children or household tasks, but with the universe!). This sensual arousal is not genital; it is part of the erotic possibilities of the body. . . .

As a graduate student I am taking a course from an extraordinary professor. This person is able to tie together many disparate historical events until I see, often with a sudden and startling clarity, their meaning. The other students and I talk about how stimulating the course is. Often I am thrilled by a particular lecture. This teacher excites my mind. But my body takes special notice for it sometimes trembles in sympathy with the excitement. Even in matters as cerebral as a history class, my embodied spirit is aroused. . . .

This emotional and sensual arousal is part of our sexuality. When we are in love, we notice nature and music in a new way. When we are lonely, a drabness darkens the landscape and robs us of the delights that usually refresh us. But if we are frightened by the surprising stirrings of our body, we may avoid *all* sensual arousals lest they lead to a loss of control.

Sexuality is, then, a more inclusive category than sex. Sexuality includes genital behavior and embraces much more that is of consequence. James Nelson captures the scope of sexuality when he says, "While our sexuality does not determine all our feelings, thoughts, and actions, in ways both obvious and covert it permeates and affects them all."

The Movement of Sexual Maturity

Sex and sexuality are not the same, but they are interrelated. Real connections exist between genetics (a determining factor in sex) and gender (a critical part of sexuality). Our emotional responsiveness and our comfort in being close to other people are linked. In fact, the erotic excitement of romance can lead to the broader commitments of mutual love. The way that we experience these connections is significant, especially to our sexual maturity.

Our experience of sex, our awareness of sexuality, our attitude toward close relationships—these all shape our sense of self. Sexual maturity is not a state that is achieved once and for all. Rather it is an ongoing process. To mature sexually is to become more confident and more comfortable with the ways that sex, sexuality, and intimacy are part of our own life. We express this maturity in many different lifestyles. The issue here is not married or single, gay or straight, celibate or sexually active. Each of these can be a gratifying and generous way to live. However, sexual maturity challenges us to develop a *pattern of life* that is rooted in the wisdom of our own experience and that is responsive to the values and commitments that give our life meaning.

In his insightful article "Reuniting Sexuality and Spirituality," James Nelson explores the connections between holiness and sexual maturing. Sanctification, he reminds us, means both wholeness and holiness. Christians today are especially eager to grow holy *in and through* their sexuality. Nelson gives some hints of the direction of this religious maturing:

> Sexual sanctification can mean growth in bodily self-acceptance, in the capacity for sensuousness, in the capacity for play, in the diffusion of the erotic throughout the body (rather than in its genitalization) . . .

Holiness—and wholeness—does not mean a flight from the sexual. It demands a befriending of this frightening but attractive force called *eros*. It requires that we become more profoundly erotic.

REFLECTIVE EXERCISE

Use the phrases below to explore your own experience of the range of sexuality. Complete the sentence begun by each phrase. There is no need to force an answer, just respond with what comes to mind at the time. For some phrases you may have several responses; others may call up little for you right now. You may find it valuable to share this exercise with a friend or in a small group setting.

When I think of myself as a sexual person, I . . .

For me, sexuality is . . .

These days, my body . . .

For me, closeness with someone of the same sex is . . .

When I wonder whether others are attracted to me sexually, I . . .

For me, sexuality and spirituality . . .

ADDITIONAL RESOURCES

James Nelson continues to make a significant contribution to the Christian reflection on sexuality; see his *Body Theology* and *Embodiment: An Approach to Sexuality and Christian Theology.* The quotation at the end of this chapter is from his article "Reuniting Sexuality and Spirituality," which appeared in *Christian Century.* In *Sexuality and the Sacred: Sources for Theological Reflection,* edited by James Nelson and Sandra Longfellow, the authors explore a range of perspectives on the integration of sexuality and spirituality.

Carlo Maria Martini, the Cardinal Archbishop of Milan, draws on scripture and the theological work of John Paul II in *On the Body: A Contemporary Theology of Sexuality.* In his article "A Disembodied 'Theology of the Body,'" Luke Timothy Johnson offers a theological critique of the pope's discussion of sexuality. Elizabeth Moltmann-Wendel examines the experience of body in the New Testament and in contemporary Christian life in *I Am My Body: A Theology of Embodiment.*

Theologian Carl Koch joins nurse Joyce Heil to provide information and prayerful exercises focusing on the body, in *Created in God's Image: Meditating on Our Body.* Tom Driver's meditation is part of his chapter "Speaking from the Body," in *Theology and the Body,* edited by John Fenton.

In *The Power of Touch,* Phyllis Davis offers a thought-provoking discussion of the importance of touch throughout the human lifespan. Anthropologist Ashley Montague explores "the human significance of the skin" in his evocative essay *Touching.* Mary Anne Finch demonstrates how these insights may be embodied in pastoral practice in *Care Through Touch: Massage as the Art of Anointing.*

4

Intimacy and Commitment

RUTH AND I HAVE WORKED IN THE SAME OFFICE now for six years. Yesterday she told me she would be leaving at the end of the month. I've known for a while that she's been thinking about this change, but it still came as a shock. I have been distracted all day, recalling the ups and downs of our time together.

When we first began to work together, I was suspicious of her. Ruth was older than I am but less experienced in our company. Which one of us would really be in charge? My suspicion quickly gave way to irritation. We had such different working styles: her quickness looked impulsive to me. I soon learned that my careful reflection seemed like foot-dragging to her!

But after about six months we began to mesh. In two years' time we have become a terrific team—able to depend on each other without a doubt or second thought. I respect her energy in approaching a problem; I've even started to show more enthusiasm myself! I know she's come to appreciate my deliberation and patience. We've learned a lot from working so closely together and had some good fun in the process. We still often disagree but our arguments feel clean; we don't need to punish or manipulate each other. Surprisingly, we spend almost no time together apart from the office. Only now do I realize how close we have become. What will I do without her?

This is not a tale of romance, but it is a story of intimacy. Intimacy is about engagement—the many ways we hold one another. In some relationships we embrace one another as lovers. But the engagements of adult life go beyond passion and romance. As friends, we hold one another in affection; as colleagues, we hold one another accountable in our work. More painfully, we often engage one another in the confusing embrace of conflict.

In this chapter we will explore the wider experience of intimacy. Sometimes the phrase "an intimate relationship" is used in a way that really means sexual sharing. But intimacy is more than a polite synonym for genital behavior. Intimacy encompasses more than sex. Intimacy brings us close. An intimate relationship draws us close enough to one another that we are changed in the process.

The relationship of friendship brings us close. We share our self with friends, and they open themselves to us in return. Friendship makes us intimates—emotional ties develop; our lives overlap. This proximity, while offering comfort and support, also makes friends our most knowledgeable critics. And dismissing the criticism of a trusted confidant is not easy. Friendship confirms our sense of self (our friends know us well and love us still!). Friendship also tests that identity, challenging us with new information and influencing the way we understand ourself.

But intimacy is not limited to emotional closeness. Collaboration brings us close. Working together puts people regularly in close contact. We see each other's strength and resilience; we learn about each other's limitations and blind spots. Even without becoming friends, we can become genuinely involved in one another's lives. This involvement is what intimacy is about.

In close relationships, however, we hold one another in conflict as often as in compassion and care. This more ambiguous embrace may be part of intimacy as well. Two friends, for example, struggle to resolve a painful misunderstanding. As the conflict develops, they feel distant from each other and dangerously exposed: "I am vulnerable here; I may be hurt." But often, as the struggle is resolved, they sense that they have grown closer. In the midst of—perhaps *because of*—the conflict, their relationship deepens. If this seems paradoxical at first, it makes sense. When we are in conflict, we are engaged with one another. This genuine engagement, more than warm feelings, makes for intimacy.

Friendship, love, collaboration, negotiation, compromise, conflict—these are the arenas of intimacy. Our embraces range from the erotic to the competitive, from the friendly to the antagonistic. These differing experiences raise the questions: Are we sure enough of our-selves to risk drawing close to someone else? Are we open to the new information that may arise as we come together? In these questions we face what frightens us most about intimacy—not what we learn about others but what we learn about ourself.

A surprising lesson of intimacy is the ambivalence we feel. Being close to other people brings both delight and annoyance. And often these two feelings exist side by side. A friend's genuine concern con-soles me, yet sometimes her interest seems meddlesome. The col-league with whom I work most effectively also makes me the most impatient.

Our ambivalence puts us in touch with the practical demands of intimacy. Drawing close, we delight in each other's company; we bring out the best in each other; we love each other well. But being close, we also offend each other and make unrealistic demands. We misinterpret each other's motives; we get in each other's way. Maturing in intimacy means learning to live with both the exhilaration and the strain that come with being close.

Personal Strengths for Intimacy

Intimacy, then, carries costs. If its rewards are great, so are its require-ments. To meet these demands requires a robust range of personal resources—strengths that we develop in the give-and-take of our rela-tionships.

What does being close to people require? In his classic studies in adult maturity, psychologist Erik Erikson has looked for answers. He uses the term *intimacy* to name a cluster of personal strengths that support our efforts to draw close to one another. What are these resources? Following Erikson's lead, we will start with a working defi-nition and then go on to explore its elements.

As a strength of adult maturity, intimacy is the capacity

- to commit ourself to particular people
- in relationships that last over time
- and to meet the accompanying demands for change
- in ways that do not compromise personal integrity.

The Capacity for Commitment

How is life to be lived well? Most of us are intrigued by the question. We recognize that our lives are likely to hold some suffering, periods of confusion or loss or pain. But we search for ways of living that—over a lifetime—will be both satisfying and effective. Satisfying: so that our life makes sense to us personally, bringing joy and meaning and peace. And effective: so that our life makes sense beyond just ourselves. We want to make a contribution, to help other people, to participate in a larger world. To live this way means to link our lives to people and to values. We do this by developing a capacity for commitment.

Philosopher Hannah Arendt captures the importance of commitment when she says: "The remedy for unpredictability, for the chaotic uncertainty of the future, is contained in the faculty to make and keep promises." Commitments rescue life from being a series of random encounters interrupting our isolation. We commit ourselves to people and to values in the hope for a fruitful life.

Personal commitment is the core strength in intimacy. In our commitments we pledge ourselves *for the future*—beyond both our vision and our control. This risk is necessary, for without commitment we limit our loyalties to the present. But this risk is also serious because we do not control the future. We cannot be certain that our present feelings will last. In a commitment, we summon our will in an effort to shape the future. We hold ourselves open to whatever is necessary so that the bond between us may endure.

As we move through life, we come to recognize two kinds of important commitments. One is the ability to commit ourself to ideals and values; without this, our life remains unfocused. The other is the ability to commit ourself to persons; without this, we remain alone.

This difference is most easily seen in the following example: At sixteen, Eileen is approaching those initial decisions about personal values that will shape her early adult years. She is an idealistic young woman, already determined to pursue a career that will enable her to use her talent to make the world better. She wants to be either a research chemist in pursuit of a cure for cancer or an agricultural specialist working in drought-stricken Africa. Eileen's idealism is appealing; it also gives evidence of her growing ability to commit herself to values—one of the decisive choices of adult maturity.

But as we learn more, we see that all is not well in her life these days. To start with, Eileen's relations with her parents are strained. Eileen thinks that they make impossible demands on her; their ideas are out-moded; they still treat her like a child. Most of her teachers, she finds, are boring. She is critical of her social world as well: none of the girls she has as friends are very popular; none of the really attractive guys are interested in her.

Learning these details of Eileen's experience can depress us: this idealistic young woman loves humanity but does not like people! In Eileen's case we may console ourselves by recalling that she is, after all, only a teenager. To love abstract humanity but to dislike most of the particular people we meet on an everyday basis—that is not a bad way to be sixteen. But it is an awkward way to be thirty-six!

In the move beyond adolescence, committing ourself to *particular* people becomes increasingly important. In the friendships and work that fill our twenties we begin to realize that "humanity" does not exist. All there is out there is people. If we are going to link our life in any meaningful way, the connection must come through commit-ment to some of the actual people we meet. But people come only in the particular; each is a lovely, if limited, instance of humanity. If life is not to be lived alone, we must be able to commit our self to these real people, limited and flawed as they may be.

This commitment "in the particular" makes demands in all close relationships. In marriage, for example, we marry both an individual and an ideal. Our partner is "perfect" for us; he has all the attributes for which we have been searching. Gradually we discover that we have not wed the ideal husband. We have married this person who has not only wonderful gifts but also fears and doubts that surprise both of us. Love matures as we commit our self not to the idealized person we married a decade ago but to *this person* right now.

A similar purification can be part of our commitment to a group—a profession, a religious congregation, a working team. We may begin with an idealized sense of the members, but soon we learn the truth. This group is composed of "just people." Like ourself, they are both capable and flawed, wounded and blessed. Unless we can link our life with people like that, intimacy will be hard to come by.

In Relationships That Last Over Time

Most of us can recall a dear friend we had in college or in the old neighborhood as we were growing up. As close as we were then, we are no longer in touch. We all know of marriages that, even though they seemed so well begun, have ended. These experiences raise questions: How long should a relationship last? How long, we wonder, does intimacy endure?

The issue of duration challenges us all. For some of us, the question is, "Can I give my heart here, if it may not be forever?" The question arises often these days, as mobility complicates relationships. In our first job, for example, we make new friends with gusto. When a job change moves us away, we feel the pain of losing these friends but we gamely set out to make new ones. After a few more moves, we become more hesitant: How long will we be here? Is getting involved really necessary? Is getting involved worthwhile?

With experiences like this, we want to strike a bargain: "Give me a relationship that is guaranteed to last and I will be open to the demands of intimacy. But anything short of that kind of guarantee is just not worth the risk." Of course, at the start of a relationship no such guarantee exists. Relationships do not come like appliances, with factory warranties. Even relationships once thought of as stable and permanent are now seen differently. We recognize more readily today that indissolubility is a graced achievement of a marriage over a lifetime, rather than an assurance at the start. In other relationships, too, loyalty and longevity are gifts of the relationship more than guarantees.

Others of us, suspicious of guarantees, try to strike a different bargain: "I am able to be present to you now but don't ask me to say 'tomorrow.' Tomorrow is too unknown. How can I pledge my future based only on what I know now? I may change, you may change, the situation between us may be different." Duration becomes the enemy here, as we draw back from establishing the links that will make a claim on our future. But without these kinds of links, we doom our life to loneliness.

Relationships cost. And some of the costs cannot be predicted or circumscribed ahead of time. To deal with the demands of duration as these emerge in our relationships, we must draw upon our resources for intimacy.

To Meet the Demands for Personal Change

Intimacy is not static. People change and relationships develop over time. Reminiscing with an old friend, we recall that when we first met we didn't even like each other! But over the years we have grown closer. Through lots of affection and not a little conflict, our friendship has blossomed in ways neither one of us could have predicted.

Relationships that last, change. Sometimes, as in the example above, we experience the changes positively. But often enough these developments seem more negative. A friendship begun with such vigor turns sour; now defensiveness replaces the openness we used to enjoy. "What has happened to us?" we lament. "You've changed and it's not fair!" These confusions can be part of our marriage: "You are not the woman I thought I married; things are not turning out the way I had hoped." Here change comes as disappointment, even betrayal. Promises have not been kept and someone is to blame.

Change makes demands—for accommodation, for understanding, for tolerance, for forgiveness. In these demands the costs of intimacy become clear. If this relationship is to continue, a price must be paid. The price is tendered in the coin of personal change. For this marriage to continue, we must set aside some of our earlier expectations and struggle toward a new understanding of who we are for one another. For a friendship to grow, we must be open to the demands that loyalty makes. If we are to become real colleagues, we will have to let our co-workers see our weaknesses as well as our strengths. Close relationships involve an overlapping of space, a willingness to be influenced, an openness to the possibility of change. To weigh and meet these demands, we must draw on our resources for intimacy.

Intimacy invites us to change. But if our sense of self is not strong, close relationships will appear not only difficult but dangerous. Then we fear getting close, because the other person may overwhelm us. Or, because we have no clear sense of who we are, we may try to become whatever the other wants us to be, or what we *imagine* this person wants us to be.

If our capacity for closeness is not rooted in some sense of our adequacy on our own, the intimacy that results will lead not to mutuality but to symbiosis. Mature intimacy, which is more than an impulse for merger, includes a sense of autonomy and an awareness of our continuing responsibility for ourself. The tension between closeness and autonomy is part of the ambivalence of intimacy. Maturity does not do away with the struggle but brings with it the resources that help us tolerate the strain.

Without Compromising Our Integrity

Intimacy often demands compromise—a willingness to come to agreement through changes on both sides. But to the purist, compromise sounds like surrender, giving in without a fight, failing to stand up for what we believe. In close relationships many of us come to see compromise in quite another light. We learn that sometimes compromise is the best way to say "I love you."

But when and how to compromise? When is compromise a gesture of generosity and when is it a failure to meet an important challenge? How do we stay open to significant change without selling ourself out?

Sometimes the challenge is clear. We need to apologize, to admit we were wrong; we need to ask forgiveness. We make the first move toward reconciliation, even though we know that our friend shares some of the blame. We may feel awkward and embarrassed, but when we move toward the other person in this way we sense growth. Compromise puts us in touch with what is best in us.

But we have all had other experiences with compromise. We have recognized that for a relationship—a marriage, a work team, a friendship—to continue, we will have to change. But this concession does not lead to growth. The accommodation asked is that we give up ourself—let go of something that is crucial to who we are or who we might be at our best. In short, for this relationship to continue we must sell out.

Many forces may incline us to make such a compromise: we don't want to disappoint others; we want to do what appears virtuous. But beneath these voices we hear the call of conscience: the price of this compromise is our integrity.

The suggestion here is not that, if we were mature, personal change would always be easy. Nor is it that, if we were mature, we could easily tell the difference between the demands for change that lead to life and those that put us at risk of losing what is best in us. What we are suggesting is that maturity brings the ability to hang in there—to tolerate the strain as we try to discern what is being asked of us and where these demands will lead.

Intimacy and Integrity: A Challenge for Women and for Men

Intimacy leads us beyond individualism but not beyond integrity. In close relationships we work out the connections between intimacy and integrity. We ask ourselves how we can share deeply with others, in ways that respect and replenish who we really are. This question confronts each of us. But, as feminist psychologists are showing us today, the challenge posed by the question is different for women than for men. The difficulty for many men involves the word *connection*. Men ask, "How can we draw close to other people in ways that do not threaten our sense of self as independent?" Women more often feel the strain of the word *separation*. They ask, "How can we nourish a sense of personal autonomy, in ways that do not diminish the important connections we have with other people?"

Psychologist Nancy Chodorow has examined child-rearing practices to help us understand the roots of this fundamental difference. Chodorow's analysis has not gone unchallenged, but many people involved in the study of gender differences continue to find her perspective persuasive.

In many cultures—ours included—mothers are the primary, sometimes the exclusive, caretakers of young children of either sex. Most often, the first emotionally close relationship that an infant experiences is with the mother. As this primary experience of love develops, a girl child comes gradually to recognize that mother is "not me" even though, as a woman, she is "like me." Her early awareness of self is as *like* mother, as connected with the loved one. The boy child grows into the realization that mother is "not me" but also "not like me." His awareness of self depends on a more profound sense of separation from the loved one.

This early developmental history influences us as adults. For many women, the sense of "who I am" comes from *connections* with other people. Relationships are thus central to a woman's identity. Closeness to other people confirms her sense of self. For many men, the sense of "who I am" comes from *separateness* from other people. For a man, emotional closeness creates tension because it challenges this separateness. Relationships, then, can be experienced as a risk to identity.

Reaffirming what all of us know from our own lives is important here. Both men and women appreciate the benefits of emotional closeness; women and men alike value the resources of personal autonomy. But in building a lifestyle that nurtures both intimacy and integrity, women and men are likely to experience different strains.

Most women find close relationships both essential and satisfying. For a woman, being close to other people confirms her womanhood (that's what women are supposed to do well) and reinforces a positive sense of self. Acting independently—that is, relying on her own resources—is desirable in many ways but is a more ambiguous achievement than connecting with others. To succeed in this autonomous stance may leave her feeling less "feminine." (Men—not women—are supposed to be good at standing apart and acting on their own!)

Succeeding in independence may threaten a woman at a more basic level. For many women the earliest sense of self is developed by drawing close, first to mother and then to others. As an adult, a woman's identity continues to be rooted in similarity and connection. Self-reliance suggests separation; this goes against the feminine sense of self as essentially connected with other people. Autonomy is then risky, for it demands differentiation, setting herself apart from others.

A comparable dynamic complicates things for men. For a man, acting independently confirms masculinity (that's what men are supposed to do well) and helps him feel good about himself. Behaving in ways that bring him close to other people adds a good deal to his life, but these benefits are not without a price. Wanting close relationships calls his manhood into question (a "real man" is able to go it alone); being successful at drawing close to others may even undermine rather than support his self-esteem. (After all, women—not men—are supposed to be good at that sort of thing!)

At a more basic level, drawing close to people may be threatening to men whose initial sense of self is developed by separation, by moving away from mother. This awareness of self is subsequently defended by developing a strong sense of the boundaries between myself and other people. Close relationships threaten these boundaries. The response of some men can be panic. Without being fully conscious of the cause of his distress, he senses that if he lets this person become close he risks more than personal preferences or his daily schedule. His very being is at stake, his sense of separate selfhood, his confident grasp of who he is as a man.

Many women interpret relationships as a source of security. For them, emotional connections form a nurturing network that supports survival and growth. A woman knows that healthy relationships include both union and separateness. Still, separateness seems risky. Her inner boundaries between self and others remain somewhat flexible, enabling her to more easily incorporate other people into the world of her awareness and concern. In her relationships, then, she acts to overcome the distance between herself and her partners. She strengthens her ties with other people; she accommodates her wishes to those of others, compromises for the sake of harmony, even acquiesces if necessary.

For most women, relationships develop holistically, sometimes cutting across the clear distinctions (boss/worker; professional/client) that preserve separateness. A woman often wants to add emotional dimensions—affection, care, mutual concern—to these otherwise "cool" relationships, so that she feels more connected.

For many men, emotional security comes from a sense of separateness. Then connections appear risky; relationships need boundaries and structures to make them safe. Close relationships, with their emotional dimensions and added demands, are most threatening. Some men deal with this risk by avoidance; they do not let themselves get close to other people. Others use control to lessen the risks; they reinforce power differences (dating only much younger women; working exclusively with junior colleagues) or insist on clear roles and rules for what goes on in the relationship. Others hold back essential parts of themselves—feelings, hopes, dreams, vulnerability, emotions—to protect a sense of separateness from their partners.

As women and as men, then, we develop—often without full awareness—characteristic responses in close relationships. When a relationship starts to require us to change, some of us flee. Our underlying attitude is that we are open to relationships so long as they don't make demands, at least not at any serious level. As soon as there is a hint that we will have to change for this relationship to continue, we leave. Even if we stay around physically, we withdraw psychologically. We remove ourself from relationships that make demands.

For others of us, the temptation is different. Faced with a demand that we change so that a relationship may continue, we give in. Many women report that this is a tendency to which they feel particularly vulnerable. Having learned early that relationships are important to her, a woman may feel that she cannot risk resisting its demands—any demand. When she realizes that she must change for the relationship to continue, she is inclined to acquiesce easily, without weighing the cost to her integrity or self-esteem.

Maturity moves us beyond these automatic responses. We can face a demand for change without running away or immediately giving in. As we struggle with our partner toward a solution that is mutually respectful and mutually satisfying, we are able to tolerate the strain.

Sex and Intimacy

Sex is not the whole of intimacy, but for many of us sex is part of our maturing in love. We have experienced the power of sexual sharing, recognizing that it can open us to a larger communion. Risking closeness in sex play, we have learned to let down our defenses in other ways as well. Our nakedness has taught us that showing the other who we really are is safe—our lover will not mock us; our beloved will not desert us. In lovemaking we share a delight that helps appease the tensions that arise—inevitably and expectably—in our continuing close contact.

Personal experience affirms the links between sex and love. This connection has made sexual love a model and metaphor of intimacy. The rituals of lovemaking highlight, in dramatic fashion, features common to other experiences of intimacy as well—the impulse to share our self with another, the anxious moment of self-revelation, the affirmation of being accepted, the delight in the give-and-take of the activities we share. Love-play is a vivid example of the "mutual regulation of complicated patterns" that characterizes intimacy, whatever its shape. The gift of new life is a profound sign of the vitality and fruitfulness of genuine love.

REFLECTIVE EXERCISE

What are the personal strengths that make intimacy possible? We have explored this question in the chapter. Now consider your own experience.

Begin by recalling the people who are your "intimates," those close to you in love or work or friendship. Take time to savor the presence of these special people in your life.

Select one of these significant relationships. Recall some of the details: the way you met, the ups and downs of your history together, what each of you brings to the relationship, how things are between you these days. Then respond to these questions.

- As you reflect on this relationship, what does it tell you about your strengths for intimacy, about the resources you bring to being close to others?

- Have you learned anything here about your limits regarding intimacy, about the frustrations and hesitancies you feel when you come close to others?

- Are there ways this relationship has helped you get better at intimacy, more confident or more comfortable in drawing close to other people?

ADDITIONAL RESOURCES

Erik Erikson and Joan Erikson discuss intimacy as a strength of adult maturity in *The Life Cycle Completed: A Review;* for an introduction to this and other of Erikson's writing, see the excellent collection *The Erik Erikson Reader,* edited by Robert Coles. Nancy Chodorow's influential analysis of the impact on gender of child-rearing patterns is found in *The Reproduction of Mothering: Psychoanalysis and the Sociology of Gender;* in *The Power of Feelings: Personal Meaning in Psychoanalysis, Gender and Culture,* she expands and clarifies her position.

Fran Ferder and John Heagle examine psychological and spiritual dynamics of intimacy in *Your Sexual Self: Pathways to Authentic Intimacy.* In *The Space Between Us: Exploring the Dimensions of Human Relationships,* Ruthellen Josselson looks at elements that are crucial in mature relationships. *The Dance of Intimacy,* by Harriet Goldhor Lerner, offers guidance for developing healthy patterns in close relationships. In *Time and Intimacy,* Joel Bennett reflects on the transcendent dimension of human relationships. Mary Durkin explores themes of sexuality and intimacy in the religious perspective in *Feast of Love: Pope John Paul II on Human Intimacy.*

Catherine Miles Wallace reflects on commitment as both challenge and gift in *For Fidelity: How Intimacy and Commitment Enrich Our Lives.* In *Living the Renewed Life,* Wayne Brown gives practical advice and encouragement for the ongoing work of honoring commitments. Robert Firestone and Joyce Catlett examine psychological barriers to closeness in adult life in *Fear of Intimacy.* We discuss the developmental characteristics of intimacy in our *Christian Life Patterns: Psychological Challenges and Religious Invitations of Adult Life.*

Part Two

Arenas of Intimacy

W E PURSUE INTIMACY ALONG MANY PATHS: friendship, collaboration in work, marriage and family life. These avenues of association often become arenas: sites of affection and a deepening
commitment. And these arenas can become crucibles: places where our
ability to love and to be faithful is painfully tested and purified.

In Part 2 we examine the arena of marriage, where sexual passions
are forged into lifelong commitments. We turn next to the hopes and
challenges of intimacy that are part of being single. Then we reflect on
the sensitive questions that surround being Christian and homosexual. Finally, we discuss the lifestyle of consecrated celibacy in the
life of the church today.

5

The Maturing of Romance in Marriage

M ANY OF US FIND INTIMACY IN MARRIAGE. Even more of us expect to find it there. As a cultural ideal, marriage holds so much promise. Most Americans, whether married or not, see marriage as the preferred setting for intimacy. No other adult relationship seems so serious or so sustained. Even those who are aware—sometimes from personal experience—of the perils that marriages face still carry images of married love that are remarkably positive.

As a result, most of us have high expectations of marriage. We want romance—the emotional and sexual attraction that will keep our love-making passionate. We want to be friends—enjoying each other's company, discovering in one another the comfort and challenge, the solace and stimulation that we need. We want devotion too—the loyalty that we can count on, the trust that we are safe in each other's care.

Marriage did not always carry such high demands. Until well into the twentieth century, wives and husbands did not generally expect to be each other's chief emotional companion or best friend. And many couples today recognize that the "companionate marriage" expands the challenges as well as the blessings of married life. Yet few among us would be satisfied with a style of marriage that did not have friend-ship and mutual devotion as major goals.

Marriage and Romance

To Americans, romance stands as the source and seal of the decision to be married. But marriage and romance have not always been bedfellows. For many centuries Christians and others knew that while marriage might lead to love, it did not necessarily start out there.

The accepted norm for marriage today is personal selection based on romantic love. The understanding is that *we choose* whom we shall marry, and the person we choose is someone with whom we have fallen in love. Across different periods and in other cultures, a range of factors have been accepted as appropriate reasons for marriage: the decision of parents, the advice of match makers, concern for dynastic purity or the effective transfer of property. Today most Americans would feel uneasy about a marriage motivated by these concerns. The sophisticated or the skeptical among us will recognize that these factors are still influential. But most of us feel that a marriage is well begun only when the spouses choose for themselves and when the choice is based, at least in large part, on a shared experience of romantic love.

The Ingredients of Romance

What goes on in romantic love? Three elements are central. The first is powerful *attraction*. Romance draws us together, physically and emotionally. Apart, we long for the other's presence; when we are near, we feel exhilarated. The allure can be overwhelming; we feel "swept away." The forces at play seem "bigger than both of us," even beyond conscious choice. We speak of the "magnetism" we feel, the "chemistry" between us. These images reflect an awareness that we are caught up in something beyond our control. In this excitement and attraction, the sexual component is strong. Lovers may choose to reserve genital expression until after the formal commitment of marriage, but sexual energy is high.

Second, romance celebrates a sense of "fit." In romantic love a strong (even if not always accurate) awareness of *congruence and compatibility* emerges. We are convinced that we are perfectly suited for one another: "we fit together well." We like the same things; we have the same hopes for our love; we agree on what is important in life. Romance, then, links us in values and vision as well as in affection and attraction.

Third, romance carries *promise for the future*. If our shared present holds such delight, surely a common future holds even more. This sense of promise fuels the decision to take on the broader commitments of married life. Romance leads us into marriage with powerful hopes of what the future will bring. Together, we want to shape a life that guarantees the love we know now and realizes our shared vision of an even richer future.

The Value of Romance

We have fallen in love: in our culture, this is how most marriages start. And, all things considered, romantic love is not such a bad place for a marriage to begin. Romance is a legitimate and important early stage of love. Sexual longing is linked with genuine concern for the other person; the seeds of mutual devotion are planted here. The powerful attraction we feel for each other moves toward commitment, encouraging us to be open to the risks and possibilities that marriage will bring. A sense of compatibility reinforces the hope that this love will last. Our dream of a shared future nurtures a *"we"* that is larger than our separate ambitions.

Romance, then, is often love's ally. It is not simply, as the cynic would say, a deception. Romance is more than just a delightful distraction, to be set aside once we become involved in the serious business of marriage. Still, romance remains ambiguous. Two proverbs capture the ambiguity. Most of us know—from our own experience and from what we see in the lives of others—that both these adages are true. "Love is blind," one proverb insists. Caught up in the excitement of romance, people can overlook even what seems obvious to others. Lovers respond selectively, sometimes blocking out what they do not want to see. Most of us have learned the sober lessons that come from being blinded by love. So we learn to be properly suspicious of love's enthusiasms, if not always in our own lives at least in our judgments about other people's affairs.

But this is not the only conviction we have about romance. Most of us know equally well that "only the lover has eyes to see clearly." When we are in love, we see things—in the person we love, even in ourselves—that are lost on others. The lover knows the truth about the beloved. In the eyes of the one who loves us we see reflected the parts of our self that we have been unable or unwilling to accept—our loveliness, our goodness, our dream.

Love is blind and love sees clearly—the romance that brings us to marriage includes both these dynamics. But how much "insight" and how much "illusion" are not immediately clear! The early years of married life test our romantic hopes against the reality of who we are and how we are together. This maturing process confirms many of love's insights and uncovers some of love's illusions. Gradually the evidence mounts: what we are experiencing is not all that we expected. These discrepancies begin to erode the euphoria of romance. The honeymoon is over.

This early disappointment marks a critical moment in a marriage. For some couples, the crisis proves fatal and moves them inevitably to divorce. For others, the marriage remains intact but the couple lose touch with the passion that once energized love. But in many marriages, love now becomes a more deliberate choice. We come to appreciate marriage as an action—something we *do together*—not just something that we are "taken up in." This realization moves us beyond the exhilarating but largely passive experience of *falling in love* toward love as a chosen and cultivated commitment.

The commitments of marriage are the promises we make—to ourselves, to one another, to the world—to do whatever is necessary for our love to grow. Our commitments, of course, do not control the future. That sober lesson we learn as we move through life. Gradually, the events of our days challenge us to give up one by one our adolescent images of omnipotence. Maturity modifies both our sense of power and our sense of control. We discover that we are both stronger and weaker than we had realized. Our promises may be fragile, but they still have force. This vulnerable strength of commitment can transform romance into a love that sustains marriage for a lifetime.

This transformation, while it need not signal the loss of romance, does point to its purification. Committed love grows as we are able to acknowledge and appreciate our spouse "as is," beyond the idealized images that may have been part of our early attraction. The challenge is not to keep on loving the person we thought we were marrying, but to love the real person we did marry! We come to know our spouse more completely and more clearly, as perhaps more gifted than we had dreamed but also as more limited than we had hoped.

Many of us come to marriage nurtured on fairytales of "happily ever after." Music lyrics and films celebrating the sexual bliss of romantic love have forcefully shaped our expectations. We may even have learned in our religious upbringing that good marriages will be free of conflict. Panic arises as these romantic images betray us. To sustain these illusions involves considerable strain, but we often have nowhere to turn for more realistic models of what marriage is or can be.

The religious rhetoric surrounding marriage can help or hinder a couple facing this purification. Imagery that pictures marriage only as an institution—a *state of matrimony* that we inhabit—does not equip us for the surprising changes in this shared journey. The greatest gift that Christian faith may have to give to a married couple is the expectation of forgiveness. The move beyond infatuation often includes false starts; the purification of romantic love forces us to face our failures. Forgiveness becomes a powerful resource for this journey. If we can summon the courage and skill to forgive and to accept forgiveness, our married romance will have a future.

Season of Struggle

Romance, as we have said, is not a bad place to begin a marriage. But a marriage cannot thrive only on romance. Early romance has gotten us to this point on the journey, but by itself it can take us no farther. In fact, romance can become a stumbling block. Trying to hold on to the good feelings that accompany our early infatuation, we look away from any evidence that contradicts these romantic ideals. Afraid that the loss of romance signals the end of our marriage, we resist this new information. Differences between us are denied, competition must be masked, conflict suppressed.

For marriage to mature, our love must expand to include bonds between us that are stronger than romance. Our early enchantment hinted at this expanded love. The purification of romance allows these broader links of love to emerge and be strengthened. But, as we are forced to face some of the illusions that are part of our relationship, purification often generates tension.

In some marriages, this is a time of recrimination. Our sense is that we have been lied to; even worse, we have lied to ourself. Much effort goes into getting our spouse to be different, to live up to the promises, hopes, illusions of romance. We may use overt and subtle power tactics (threats, accusations, silence) to buttress these demands. We may withhold affection, using sex as a power ploy between us. Or we may become bitter and spiteful, trying to get back at our partner for the disappointments and hurts (real and imagined) we are experiencing.

For both women and men, the reassessment of our marriage is a time of challenge, questioning, and change. But often, husband and wife are on a different timetable. One of us may move into disillusionment while the other is trying hard to hold on to the illusions. A friend of ours, whose divorce stunned us all, gave this example: "The first year I said, 'There's something wrong,' and she said, 'No, there isn't.' The second year I said, 'There's something wrong,' and she said, 'I don't think so.' The third year she said, 'Something is wrong' and I said, 'Yes, but it's too late.'"

But for many marriages, reassessment brings not disillusionment (with the emotional trauma this term suggests) but de-illusionment. Romantic love, after all, is a kind of enchantment. Enthralled by one another, we delight in every detail and mannerism. *This person*, we are convinced, can rescue us at last—from our parents, from a dull life, even from our self.

Romance often involves falling in love with love. Part of what we see in the other person is our ideal of "man" or "woman," especially of the woman or man we want to marry. This vision, partly a statement of our values and partly an expression of our needs, energizes us toward the commitments of marriage. But if enchantment starts us out on the journey of love, the route to maturity often goes by way of disenchantment. As we live together, our larger-than-life ideals come under closer scrutiny. We realize that our partner doesn't correspond perfectly to this romantic vision. The prince (or princess) does not always turn into a frog, but experience begins to challenge idealized expectations.

De-illusionment brings the mellow realization that giving up some of these illusions of early romance is safe. We now recognize many of our initial assumptions about marriage as burdens we have shouldered unnecessarily. Now we are glad to let them go. Other assumptions we had—about who each of us is, about what we could expect from each other, about what our marriage would be like—seem silly now. We have simply outgrown them. Some of our romantic illusions, we know, were genuinely useful to us. They helped get us this far together, but we do not need them any more. A stronger basis for our continuing love now exists—our growing ability to commit ourselves to each other as we actually are.

Transference and Projection

The assumptions we bring to marriage sometimes have more complicated origins. Some of us choose a marriage partner as part of a larger effort to deal with troublesome issues we faced in our original families. We use our mate to act out the other half of an old and still unresolved conflict with a parent. The unspoken, often unconscious, hope is that "this time we will get it right." For example, we may still bear in our heart the wounds of being too controlled by our mother. Her embraces always meant restraint: she often held us back or held us down. This confusion of intimacy and control still rankles. In the close contact of marriage, we experience the echoes of this constraint. We feel the threat of suffocation whenever our spouse draws close, whether in affection or in anger.

This pain, inherited from our family of origin and still harbored in our heart, makes us push away from a spouse's efforts of intimacy and closeness. The trouble, of course, is that this problem is not really "out there" between us and our mate; the problem exists "inside," in the painful memories that still surround our earliest experiences of intimacy. Trying to rework the troublesome issue, we deal with our marriage partner *"as if"* our spouse were our parent. But, in fact, our partner is not our parent. Our spouse is a unique person, responding to us here and now. To use our spouse as a stand-in for our parent, then, we must react to our mate selectively. We must focus on the qualities in our partner that remind us of our parent; we have to deny those characteristics that are genuinely different. Psychologists call this process *transference.*

Transference distorts relationships. The unfinished business of our emotional past intrudes into the present, screening out whatever does not fit the old pattern. In transference, "then and there" overshadows "here and now." When we push away from intimacy with our spouse, we are really trying to push our parent away. An "absent other" intrudes into our relationship and threatens its survival. This distortion can occur not only in marriage, but in any significant relationship.

Another psychological process may be at work between us, imperiling our efforts to move beyond the illusions of romance. This is the dynamic of *projection.* Projection is rooted in a serious discomfort with the inner world of our own emotions. We find unacceptable some part of our self—our anger or our neediness or our desire for independence. To feel good about ourself, we must not have this experience. When the feeling arises, we cannot acknowledge it as our own. So, we project the feeling onto someone else. That is, we respond to the feeling (which is really our own) as though it belonged to another person.

An example may help. A woman cannot admit a growing anger toward her husband, because "being angry" is unacceptable to her. To admit that she feels anger, especially toward a loved one, would diminish her sense of self-worth: she's not that kind of person! At a deeper level, her childhood experience may have taught her that to be angry with a loved one is dangerous. The loved one (in this early case, an all-powerful parent) can withdraw love and protection, leaving the angry child vulnerable and alone. This memory remains, though seldom at a conscious level. And this memory carries a message—anger is a threat to her well-being.

So, when her anger arises toward her husband, this woman feels the threat even more urgently than the anger. To contain the threat, she must repudiate the anger. She withdraws emotionally from her husband, hoping her angry feelings will go away. This strategy is likely to increase the tension and distance between them. But now she can identify the source of the strain outside herself: "My husband is so withdrawn and hostile these days, and it frightens me."

Projection defends this woman from unacceptable emotion by distorting her experience. The distortion happens in two steps. First, she "splits off" any conscious awareness of her anger, since she judges that this emotion is bad. Second, she projects her anger onto her spouse. Now she can identify the problem: it is his! Dealing with anger in him is less threatening than having to face it as part of her own experience.

The problem here, of course, is that it is *her* anger that is causing her trouble. Dealing with it vicariously, through her spouse, is unlikely to be of any help since the real conflict is *inside her,* not *between them.* But by refusing to recognize her own difficulty in dealing with the anger she feels, she is likely to create a problem between the two of them as well.

In intimate relationships such as marriage and close friendship, transference and projection seldom happen on one side only. For the distortions to continue, we must both participate. In *Intimate Partners,* Maggie Scarf offers moving examples of the "trade-off of projections" that develop as spouses use one another to rework inner conflicts held over from their original families. The spouses "collude" with one another to reproduce in their own marriage the problems each brings from the family of origin. What most often results from this unconscious collusion is a continuing pattern of conflict. The tension between them remains unresolved, since the husband, for example, will never become the father his wife wanted but didn't have, and she can never finally make up for the mother who did not love him enough. And since the spouse is not the real cause of the inner tension that either of us feels, the conflict is basically unresolvable. We hold each other captive in a vicious cycle of familiar but unsatisfying interactions. Marriage therapists call this pattern "the game without end." It is also a game without winners.

To end this destructive pattern we must change the rules of the game. This process starts in the realization that neither of us is an "innocent victim" here. Each of us must acknowledge our part in the collusion. We will have to deal with the hurts we carry from the past, recognizing they are *ours*. We must start to take responsibility for our own feelings and needs, rather than forcing them out of awareness or focusing them on the other person. As we come to recognize our captivity to the wounds of "then and there" we will be better able to appreciate the hope of "here and now." This relationship can be different because this relationship *is* different. We are not held hostage to our emotional histories. Change is possible; we can learn to hold one another in new, more life-giving ways.

Now our marriage becomes a place of healing. Love's power is released as we start to separate this relationship from the projections of the past. Marriage can be a relationship of injury and pain, as many of us know. But marriage can also be a place of great healing. Marriage is where most of us learn our most profound lessons of forgiving and being forgiven. We even learn how to forgive ourselves.

Beyond the Struggle

The maturing of romance often includes a time of reassessment. In some marriages this takes the shape of "the calm after the storm." Tired of the constant tension and conflict between us, we strike a truce. We are not yet really at peace, but we have determined to stop fighting. Our insistent efforts to change each other have failed; we need time to catch our breath, to let some of the wounds heal. Through stalemate, our relationship moves into a kind of stability. Weary of the struggle, we resolve, "I'm not going to continue to give more than I get in this relationship. I haven't been able to get you to change—to be different, to meet my needs, to come up to my expectations. But what I can do is set limits on what you ask of me. This is the bargain: I won't continue to make demands on you, but in return I will give only this . . . and no more." Marriage therapist Susan Campbell calls this "the contract of limited expectations."

But most of us find such a standoff unsatisfying. Surely marriage must mean more than this! Wary and exhausted, we back away from demands that our partner be different. This is less a time of passivity than of "active pacifism." We start to assume more responsibility for our self and, especially, for the expectations we have been carrying of our spouse and of our marriage. As we explore what *in our self* needs to be different, our gaze turns inward. For many women, especially, the reassessment of marriage is part of a midlife dynamic of individuation. We step back from the emotional commitments and close relationships that, as women, we have found so central to our awareness of who we are. We need time and emotional distance, so that we can savor the internal resources of integrity—our own needs and values and hopes.

This period of personal assessment marks another critical point in marriage. We must decide if our relationship is worth the work involved. We ask ourselves, "Am I willing to invest the necessary energy to come to a new relationship with my spouse, one less crippled by unreal expectations, one more shaped by who we really are? Am I willing to be open to the kind of personal examination and change that may be demanded?"

Many marriages move from a romantic experience of excitement and youthful generosity through this more cautious sense of commitment. Often this transition coincides with the exhausting years of child rearing. Burdened by career responsibilities and family demands, we learn about false expectations and genuine limits. Marriage research indicates that many couples emerge from the family years into a new experience of intimacy. Forgiveness seasons our affection. As spouses we are now more comfortable with the balance of strength and weakness we find in one another—and in ourselves.

This movement often includes an appreciation of the paradoxes of our relationship, the parts of one another that we both love and hate. We say, only half in jest, "You are so wonderfully dependable, and sometimes it drives me crazy!" Or, "Your sense of humor delights me, but must you always turn everything into a joke?" And, "I love being able to count on your love but sometimes I wish I didn't need you so much."

The paradox deepens as we recognize how interrelated these experiences are; we cannot have one side—the "good" side of the paradox—without embracing the other side. We begin to appreciate that this is the way reality comes: strength and weakness together, disappointment and delight as parts of a more complex affection that binds us to one another. Our marriage is rooted in this paradoxical strength, the love of these two flawed persons, lovely and limited as we are. This realization takes us beyond truce and stalemate into a covenant of grace.

The Authority of Our Marriage

Over many years we sort out the expectations that have haunted our marriage. As we reexamine the demands of our family and culture and religion, we begin to enter into the authority of our marriage. We are not jettisoning these cultural and religious values, but we are personalizing them.

In our early years of marriage, our parents were important authorities. Whether we chose to imitate or oppose our parents' relationship, their marriage still powerfully influenced the shape of our own. In those early years we were still susceptible to cultural imperatives: how a good wife "should" act; what a responsible husband is "supposed" to do; what a "happy family" looks like. Gradually we come to *our way* of being together. We decide to have this many children; we allot family tasks and household chores this way; we make these value choices about the use of our time and money. Slowly we craft the particular shape of our marriage. We become the authors of this commitment. We enter into the authority of our love. This can be a scary notion if we understand authority solely as an external force that belongs to leaders and to the law. But, in truth, our conscientious decisions over several decades of our marriage make us authorities too. We do not simply repeat the ideal of marriage. We give our marriage its special shape. This is the authorship of our marriage.

As we mature into the special authority of our marriage, the "we" of our commitment comes into clearer focus. Gradually we accept the truths of our shared journey: we are in this together; our spouse is not the enemy; we both want this marriage to continue, to grow. Both of us are responsible for the troubles we have experienced, both of us will have to be involved for our marriage to survive and succeed.

This purification of romance is expected—even inevitable—in marriage. But the loss of love is not. Recognizing that the quality of our commitment will change does not mean that we must fall out of love. Instead romantic love expands to include the strengths of mutual devotion. This maturing love of choice is strong enough to sustain us in the moments of strain and confusion that are part of our ongoing life together.

The experience of mutual devotion is the fruit of a maturing covenant. But the word *devotion* can be vague. What does it mean? Devotion is the feeling that is aroused as we look across the table at a spouse with whom we have shared our life for decades. We have stood by this person in illness and in anger, in childbirth and in the tedium of dressing toddlers. The feeling that stirs in us is different from youthful passion; it is a sense of *being with*. We belong with this person more profoundly than we had realized before.

In devotion, the "active" and "receptive" sides of love merge in an experience of both caring and being cared for. We are together deeply, and we each feel this is a strength. In our awe at this unexpected gift we confess, "You know me so well, and still you love me. You care for me in ways that go beyond what I could ask for. You call me out to what is best in myself. I know you hold my life as important as your own. And all these gifts I give to you as well."

Sexual Maturing in Marriage

The commitment of marriage, while it matures into a love that is larger than romance, remains a love in which affection and sexuality are central. We approach sexual maturity in our marriage as we develop our capacity to share physical affection and erotic pleasure. Sexual maturity, too, is more a process than a state, for learning to be good lovers takes time.

To give ourselves to this process of sexual maturing we must each move beyond the experience of love-play and intercourse as chiefly competitive—an experience of proving our self as a "real" woman or man or winning out over our partner. These interpretations of sex keep the focus on our self and make mutuality difficult. And without mutuality, sex is often a barrier to intimacy.

In contrast to many marriages of previous generations, couples today generally approach marriage with greater awareness of their own bodies and with more information about the details of sexual performance. Although a boon to marriage, this intellectual sophistication is more the starting point of a satisfying sex life than its guarantee. Married sex is a process through which we both learn to contribute to what is, for us, a mutually satisfying sexual experience. We learn the physical and emotional nuances that make lovemaking special for us. We develop the patterns of expression that fit us—patterns of frequency, of time and place, of initiation and response. We discover the ways in which passion and affection, humor and intensity, play a part in our own love life.

The exhilaration of sexual discovery is usually strong early in marriage, at least if we are able to move beyond an initial embarrassment. For most of us, our spouse gives us the gift of knowing that our sexuality is beautiful. Loving us in our body, our partner invites us beyond the shame we still carry. Together we can explore our passion and expose our vulnerability and self-doubt. Having risked the self-revelation of sex—and survived—we can approach with greater confidence the other, even more threatening, process of self-disclosure upon which the quality of our life together will depend.

After this early period of exploration, our sexual life can begin to level off. We have found a pattern that works for us. But, especially in the press of the other responsibilities of our lives, this pattern may become routine.

Only gradually do we realize that, although our love is strong, our lovemaking somehow falls short. An aura of romance surrounded our early sexual sharing. Frequently this romantic aura made our experiences of sex more satisfying than our lovemaking skills would otherwise justify! Now sex has lost its savor. We know that the substance of our love is more important than our sexual style, but the questions of sexual style and satisfaction become important.

American culture's current interest in sexual techniques reinforces this concern over our sex life. We are more aware of the richness of human sexuality and of the diversity of sexual expression. This new awareness can work destructively, setting up yet another standard of success against which to evaluate our own intimacy. But our expanded awareness need not have this negative effect. Instead it can remind us that the patterns of mutually satisfying sexual experience differ from couple to couple and that only *we* can best discover which pattern is best for us. In sex, as in most other aspects of marriage, to be mature does not mean to fit some general criterion of performance but to have a developing (and, perhaps, changing) sense of what is appropriate *for us*, what works *for us*.

Sex research shows the contribution that diversity and surprise make to long-term sexual satisfaction. This realization can be liberating, inviting us to expand the ways in which we celebrate the sexuality of our marriage. A sense of exploration can help us move beyond a point of boredom or routine and stimulate our own creativity in lovemaking. The expanding literature of sexual functioning can assist this process of sexual maturity in marriage, not by giving us a norm of what is "best" but by providing information that can enrich our own experimentation and choice.

Information about the normal problem areas in sexual function can also be of special help in marriage. Often, as many therapists know, sexual dysfunction is a presenting problem that points to deeper troubles around intimacy in a marriage. But real changes in sexual function, many of them the result of normal processes of aging, can disrupt a previously satisfying pattern of physical lovemaking. A husband who begins to find that maintaining an erection is difficult or a wife who starts to experience pain in intercourse may be confused, even frightened by this disquieting development. Too embarrassed to bring up the symptom for discussion, a spouse may simply avoid lovemaking. This one-sided and often unexplained decision cannot fail to affect the intimacy of the marriage! A couple's commitment to marriage for a lifetime finds a strong ally in a physician or psychological counselor who can provide information and assistance at this time. Those of us concerned about marriage—our own or other people's—should stay current with this now readily available information about sexual functioning throughout the lifespan.

The Covenant of Marriage

The image of covenant illumines Christian convictions about matrimony. From the beginning Christians and Jews were quick to compare the marriage relationship with the covenant between God and humankind. This covenant, a commitment of unconditional love, combined enormous affection with great responsibility. The covenant is a lifelong gift exchange between lovers.

Soon, however, Christians felt the cultural pressure to see marriage in a different light. This important social commitment, on which property transfer and future heirs depended, needed legal status with clearly defined rules. Therefore, marriage was best pictured as a contract. Church law, following this cultural interest in contracts, began to neglect the imagery and vocabulary of covenant. Instead, the precise, unromantic vocabulary of a contract was generated. Christian marriage became a matter of rights and duties. This commitment was legally binding if the two parties were baptized—whether or not they evidenced genuine faith; this contract was consummated in the first act of intercourse—whatever the dispositions of the spouses.

Then, in the revolutionary changes initiated by the Second Vatican Council, the imagery of covenant returned. Catholics began, again, to picture their love commitments as the exchange of gifts, more than legal rights and moral duties. In such a vision, a vital faith life becomes more important than a ritual baptism in childhood; a mature self-giving in love becomes more important than physical consummation. Christian marriages are faithful covenants of human love, rooted—as sacraments—in the enduring commitment of our gracious God.

REFLECTIVE EXERCISE

Recall a marriage that you know well—your own or your parents' or that of close friends. Be patient as you let your memory move over what you know of the course of this relationship: the early attraction, the decision to wed, the movements of life and love since that time. Then consider the maturing of romance in this marriage.

Early romance involves three ingredients: strong attraction, a sense of compatibility, a shared hope for the future. How were the elements of romance alive in this marriage? Be as concrete as you can; give examples.

Can you identify the dynamics of purification in this marriage? Perhaps a season of struggle? A time for letting go of illusions, even for disillusionment? What demands did this purification of love make on the couple? How was their relationship strengthened? Were there ways the relationship was wounded?

Is romance part of this relationship now? In what ways? Again, be as concrete as you can, giving examples of the seasoned face of romance as it enlivens this marriage today.

ADDITIONAL RESOURCES

In *Let's Make Love,* Jack Dominian continues his insightful contribution to the understanding of contemporary marriage; see especially his discussion of the spiritual significance of marital sex. Mary Anne Oliver examines the primacy of mutual love in the Christian tradition on marriage in *Conjugal Spirituality.* Patrick and Claudette McDonald explore the spiritual practices that support love in *Marital Spirituality: The Search for the Hidden Ground of Love.* In *Perilous Vows: Marital Spirituality and the Domestic Church,* Richard Gaillardetz discusses marriage and parenthood as relationships that call us into radical Christian living.

Maggie Scarf offers an instructive, if sober, look at the complex dynamics of marriage in *Intimate Partners: Patterns in Love and Marriage. Good Marriage: How and Why Love Lasts,* by Judith Wallerstein and Sandra Blakeslee, reports findings from research into what successful marriages have in common; see also John Gottman, *Why Marriages Succeed or Fail.* In *Passionate Marriage,* David Schnarch examines the role of love, sex, and intimacy in nurturing and expressing marital commitment. Carolyn and Philip Cowan show how becoming a family shapes the experience of marriage in *When Partners Become Parents.* Kathleen Fischer and Thomas Hart offer insight on ways to enhance intimacy in *Promises to Keep: Developing the Skills of Marriage.*

Drawing on Hebrew scripture and New Testament sources, Edward Schillebeeckx develops the theological background for a Christian appreciation of marriage in *Marriage: Human Reality and Saving Mystery.* In "Papal Ideals, Marital Realities," Christine Traina examines recent church statements in light of the contemporary experience of marriage. Lief Kehrwald offers a helpful discussion in *Marriage and the Spirituality of Intimacy.* In *Perspectives on Marriage,* editors Kieran Scott and Michael Warren have collected a wide range of reflections on Christian marriage today; included here are several chapters from our own earlier discussion of marriage in *Marrying Well: Stages on the Journey of Christian Marriage.*

6

More than Single

CHRISTIANS MODEL THEIR LIVES on a person who was single. The Gospels record that Jesus was not married; he took no public vow of celibacy. He was simply single. And he was more than single. Strong personal relationships and generous concern for other people distinguished his life. So fierce was his fidelity that he laid down his life for his friends.

These days being a single follower of Jesus has its hazards. A friend who teaches in a secondary school shares this experience:

> I start out each day feeling pretty good about myself and my life. But sometimes by the time I get home at night, I'm really depressed. Throughout the day people are asking me questions that seem to suggest something is wrong! Have I met anyone yet? How come I'm not dating seriously? Why am I working at that dead-end job? Am I planning to join a religious congregation? If not, why am I "still single"?

The voice of single people—those who have not married, those who are widowed or divorced—is often muted in the community of faith. With so much parish activity focused on the family and the education of children, those who are not married can feel excluded. The concerns of single people are seldom directly addressed in the religious context; even more rarely is their religious experience consulted. When the church does speak explicitly to lay people who are not married, the issue is often sexual and the tone moralistic—even punitive. Its message seems to suggest that, especially for women, "outside marriage there is no salvation."

Our goal in this chapter is to give voice to the experience of single Christians. Priority is given to statements by single people—friends, colleagues, participants we have met through our workshops. We do this, first, to recognize the limits of our own knowledge. Only recently, and with some prompting, have we begun to give serious consideration to many of the themes in this chapter. More importantly, we want to acknowledge our indebtedness. We are grateful to many people who have—with both candor and grace—helped us come to a deeper appreciation of the shape of their lives.

All around us today we hear about singles. More and more adults are living alone. Americans today tend to marry later than they did a generation ago (the Census Bureau reports that the percentage of Americans in their thirties who have not married has more than doubled in the last quarter-century). An increasing number of people do not marry at all (current estimates are that the number of adults who remain unmarried throughout their lives will soon exceed ten percent of the U.S. population). Others become "single again" through divorce or the death of the spouse.

These changing percentages are seldom reported as neutral facts. Some see the increase in a positive light. Trendy magazines tout the advantages of the single lifestyle. Housing, vacations, social clubs are offered "for singles only." Economists point out that the spending habits of single working people contribute to robust retail sales. Others interpret the data more negatively, emphasizing that the largest groups of the "new poor" in our country are older people living alone and single women with small children in their care. And those with more affluent lifestyles, as well, sometimes find cause for concern in the increase in singles. A few years back panic ran through the heart of many young career women (and their parents!) as figures appeared suggesting that—statistically speaking—a woman still single in her late thirties was more likely to be involved in a terrorist incident than to marry. (Surely only the cynical asked what the difference would be!?)

For all its prevalence, the notion of *single* is in trouble. The term groups together people who in fact are very different. A recently divorced woman living with her preschool children, a seventy-year-old widower in an affluent seniors' condominium, a twenty-six-year-old graduate student still living with his parents, a woman in her fifties with a successful career who has been on her own for some thirty years. The lifestyles of these people have little in common, and none matches the media version of the swinging single. The diversity is so great among those who are lumped together under the category *single* that dropping the term is probably a better—and certainly a more accurate—approach to this discussion. But the term is unlikely to be replaced soon. We will try, however, to be sensitive to the limitations of the word as we use it ourselves.

Into the Box

> Being single is . . . a technicality. Yes, I am the one responsible for getting things done. Nobody else will pay the bills, do the groceries, fold the laundry, change the oil, buy new tires. But those are external ways in which I'm single. In terms of who I am, being single has very little to do with it. Single is not part of my identity; I don't wake up and say to myself, "I am single." But I do wake up and say, "I am Christian." (Actually, my exact words are "good morning, God," but you get the point!) I don't walk to work knowing that I am single. But I do walk to work knowing that I am a woman. Christian? YES! Woman? YES! Single? Oh, now that you mention it, yes.

This comment by a friend of ours in her thirties is echoed frequently by others with whom we have talked. One of the problems with the term *single* is that it is a social classification more than a self-description. "Being single" is a mental category, something we construct in our minds. Because categories help us make sense of the complexity of the world, they are useful. But categories also distort. When we classify, we simplify; we group together things that are in many ways different. This makes categories dangerous, especially when we use them to describe people.

Categories are dangerous because they are always partial. When we put a person in a particular category, we ignore all the other factors that make up the person. Using a category may blind us to what is most important about the person. This is perhaps easiest to see with categories that carry a strongly negative connotation, such as "cancer patient" or "unemployed" or "alcoholic." But other classifications can also blind us. Identifying people as "Southerners" or "suburbanites" or "senior citizens" may be accurate and still not say anything very significant. In addition, the process of classification is often external to the persons being categorized. People usually do not assign themselves to a category; others do this *to* them. A colleague's explanation may make this distinction clear:

I'm always surprised when I realize people think of me as single. It's true that I am not married and that I live alone. But I rarely think about that in any explicit way. "Being single" is as little a part of my sense of myself as "having blue eyes"; as a statement of fact, it's accurate enough, but it has little to do with who I am.

Thus, being single is more an external classification than an aspect of personal identity. Many people who fit the definition do not describe themselves that way. When people do use it to describe themselves, the sense is often negative. Consider the anomaly of the singles club: Most people join a singles club in the hope that it will help them become "un-single"!

The category of *single* stumbles at the start, since it defines people by what they *are not*: singles are un-married. In *Loving Relationships*, Robert Shelton reminds us that this way of thinking has things the wrong way around:

After all, we are all born single; even if we marry, we spend from sixteen to thirty or more years single before we enter into marriage, and may well spend many more years in one or more states of being single after that. We could, in fact, think of marriage as being "un-single," rather than submitting without thinking to the common practice of labeling those who are single as "unmarried."

While the phrase "being single" does not carry much content, it does carry negative connotations. The meaning of *single* expands to include some of society's subtle prejudices: those on their own are uncommitted, irresponsible, ungenerous. An attorney in her forties relates her frustration: "It's getting harder for me to respond civilly to people who say they envy my 'uncommitted' life. I am committed—to the gospel, to my friends, to my work!"

However, despite its distortions, the category of *single* is not likely to disappear. As more and more Americans live in one-person households, the term has become important in demographic analysis. The category is also important in economic analysis, as manufacturers and advertisers identify the goods and services needed by people living alone. But *single* is not just a description; it has become a cultural image. The term *being single* is loaded with certain expectations, a set of social "shoulds." These social imperatives tell a single person how to act (the sexy single with a self-indulgent lifestyle) and what to want (the single person as conspicuous consumer, with no dependents— financial or emotional).

For a more accurate sense of what being single means, we will draw on the experiences that have been shared with us. We look first at several concerns that single people often raise. Then we turn to a broader discussion of vocation and lifestyle.

Issues in Living Alone

Single people voice particular concerns. Our friends and colleagues have emphasized several interrelated themes: self-reliance, loneliness, work, sexuality. Self-reliance can be a special gift of being single. A divorced man finds, to his amazement, that he can survive as a single parent. In the midst of the demands made on him, he discovers unexpected strengths of patience and nurturance. A woman who has grown up with a sense that "girls need to be protected" comes to recognize that her own resources are considerable; she can manage very well on her own. But such self-reliance is not always an uncomplicated achievement, as a friend in her late thirties notes:

> As a single person I constantly live with the tension between self-reliance and dependency. One of the real joys of my life has been learning that I can survive and flourish "on my own." But at the same time, I have a deep need to be connected to others, to be loved and cared for as well as to give of myself. Too much self-reliance leads me into isolation and a "lone ranger" mentality. Too much dependence leads me to feel lonely and unfulfilled. It's a tension I hold delicately these days.

Like married folk, singles struggle to balance independence and a sense of belonging. Those who live alone usually have less of the built-in companionship that many married people take for granted. As a result, single people often give more explicit attention to their relationships. For some this feels like a burden:

> In the past few years I've become aware of how much work is involved in staying in touch with my friends. I think most single people would agree. Real friendship takes a lot of time and energy. Even a casual evening with people I like seems to involve a lot of planning. Sometimes I resent the fact that I have to take so much initiative.

Most single people we know are quick to mention that having strong ties with their family and friends is very important to them. Many acknowledge that initiating and maintaining close relationships takes real effort. But more often they focus on the rich benefits that these friendships bring to people living alone. The rewards make the effort worthwhile. And important relationships are not always studied and planned. A colleague in his thirties appreciates the spontaneity he feels with friends:

> I'm single, but I'm not a loner. It means a lot to me when my married friends let me know that I'm welcome at their homes; for example, I can feel free to stop by for supper unannounced.

The care devoted to eating is an important element of an adult lifestyle and can be an intriguing indicator of one's sense of self-worth. Observers of the single lifestyle would have us look to the kitchen. Is the refrigerator stocked with a range of healthy food? Does the person take care and time to prepare a meal for "just me"? An empty refrigerator and a habit of never preparing a meal for oneself suggest an unhappiness with one's own life. Our colleague explains this phenomenon:

> I've come to see that when I start eating poorly or always eating out I'm really protesting my singleness. When I'm comfortable with myself I nourish myself, with good food and other ways too. I rely on friends and, sometimes, on fast food. But I can also care for myself; this is part of my self-reliance and self-acceptance as a single person.

Loneliness

"I like my life, but loneliness is a real problem for me." In saying this, a friend in his early thirties voices a concern shared by many people who live alone. Without a spouse and most often without children, single people face the fact of their solitariness more frequently. A colleague, successful at fifty in his career as a therapist, observes, "However exciting my workday is, I still come home alone." A writer finds that, despite many friends, her work finds her often alone and sometimes lonely. But most people who live alone recognize that loneliness is not a concern only for them. A woman in her twenties remarks:

> Loneliness is an issue for me, but I'm not sure that makes me different from other women my age. Married women can be lonely; vowed religious can be lonely. From the divorced people I've met at work I've learned that marriage is no lifetime guarantee against being lonely.

A divorced mother of four teenagers agrees: "I was much lonelier during the twenty years of my marriage than I am now!"

Loneliness is as much about how we are with ourselves as about how we are with others. People who live alone often develop personal strategies to help them deal more effectively with this everyday demon. A friend in her sixties confides:

> There are things I've learned to do when I feel lonely. I refuse to turn on the television just to have the sound of voices in the apartment. Feeling sorry for myself just makes things worse. Instead I do something to treat myself as I would a good friend: buy flowers, spend time to prepare a nice meal, settle in to read a book I've been looking forward to. Most of all I remind myself that this sorry mood will pass!

Beyond that, many people who live alone have come to recognize loneliness as more than a "problem." It can be seen as a positive signal, alerting us to examine ourselves and our relationships. A friend in his early forties acknowledges:

> I've come to realize that for me loneliness is an opportunity to learn about my intimacy needs, to help me clarify and get more realistic about my expectations of marriage.

Work

Work is of concern to most adults—married or single, women or men. The kind of work we do determines a lot about our adult identity, from the practical issues of income to the subtler questions of social worth and self-esteem. Evidence suggests that these work-related questions are of special relevance to single women.

In *Life Prints,* social scientists Grace Baruch and Rosalind Barnett and journalist Caryl Rivers report the findings of a wide-ranging study of women approaching midlife. Included in the study was a large group of women between ages thirty-five and fifty-five who had never married. The authors' discussion of their attitudes toward work makes great reading, confounding much of what is accepted as conventional wisdom about the fate of unmarried women. Based on an analysis of factors that contributed positively to the lives these women, the researchers conclude that

> the sources of well-being in the single life are not mysterious and unreachable but are in large part within the control of the woman herself. Since a life of "drift" can cost her dearly, the unmarried woman should take care to get involved in a job that she finds challenging, where she can advance, and where she can earn a good salary.

Employment in the workplace is one of the characteristic ways in which an adult identity is established. However, this means of testing and developing an adult identity has often been unavailable to young women. In past decades many women married just after completing their high school or college education. Thus they had no young adult involvement in the world of work or career. Many of those women who did work in their late teens or twenties saw this as a period of "waiting to be married" more than as a period of personal investment in a project that had a meaning of its own. Thus work did not establish identity; rather it was a stopgap, something to do until the "right" man came along.

Today both pragmatic and psychological factors influence women to delay marriage until they have tested themselves in the world of work. A look at the contemporary scene yields the pragmatic reasons for this. Today most women in the United States work in paid employment. In well over half of American families both wife and husband work outside the home. In most of these families, especially in the face of economic uncertainty, two paychecks are needed to maintain the standard of living. Every year thousands of women who are divorced or widowed find themselves suddenly responsible for their own economic well-being and, often, for that of their children as well. Women head ninety percent of the nearly five million single-parent families in our country. Pragmatically then, a woman today needs to obtain not only the education but the subsequent work experience that will enable her to support herself and, quite possibly, others as well.

But an even deeper reason moves many women to seek employment. A job is a vehicle of self-expression and self-transcendence. In the course of our work we find out and affirm who we are. We also learn how to engage ourselves in broader issues, to involve ourselves in questions of public concern. An experience of financial independence and work autonomy can be crucial to the psychological development of women, many still socialized to evaluate themselves primarily in terms of their relationships—who they are with and who wants to be with them. Work involvement helps young adults develop greater self-awareness and confidence. These psychological assets are valuable, for women and for men, whether one's future includes marriage or not.

Sexuality

Another genuine concern for singles is sexuality. Several questions arise: For Christians, is singleness necessarily equivalent to celibacy?

(In French, the word for single is *celibataire*.) Is the sole meaning of sex to be found in reproduction? If not, how does a single Christian share this pleasure in a responsible and fruitful way? But Christian circles seldom encourage these questions.

In a world that defines responsible adulthood preeminently in terms of marriage and family, a single person never quite belongs. Such an individual is likely to be seen as waiting to marry or as failing to marry. In either case, the single woman is a special worry. An unattached woman floats between the socially acceptable roles of daughter and wife. She is not accounted for. As one social commentator has observed, the single woman is "socially indigestible."

Traditionally women have been encouraged to understand themselves in terms of relationships: I am daughter, wife, mother. Thus the interpersonal relationship of marriage came to figure very prominently in the identity of women. Marriage and especially motherhood were what women *were for*. To have children, to nurture life, to care for others—these were the concerns of a woman. Her highest privileges and weightiest responsibilities were rooted here. Not to be married, not to have children was to be "unfulfilled as a woman." In the double standard of society and Christianity, a man could be excused from marriage and parenting because of some important social calling (as doctor, scientist, or priest). But for a woman not to be a mother was not to be fully woman.

If this negative evaluation of single women seems dated, consider the subtle ways it still survives. The social status of a single man is often positive; as an available escort, he is even in demand. The social status of a single woman is interpreted in different ways, often as a threat or an embarrassment. A friend notes:

> It amazes me that there is still such concern to "balance" me at a party. It's not true among my close friends, but in many social situations I am aware that a single man has to be added to the party or I can't be included. It seems there can be an "extra" man or two without any problem, but an "extra" woman breaks the etiquette.

In other settings, the unmarried woman is "sexually available." A woman in her late twenties shares her experience:

> This past year I've dated four men, two are Catholic. One goes to church every Sunday, the other almost every Sunday. Both wanted me to have sex with them on our first date. These guys wouldn't be willing to change a flat tire for me, but they expect me to be willing to sleep with them.

The traditional cultural and religious remedy for a woman's singleness is to get her married. But what if she chooses to remain single? With little support from culture or religion, single women—and men—are often left alone as they struggle to find trustworthy guidelines to shape a mature sexual lifestyle.

The Gay and Lesbian Experience

Another challenge faces lesbian and gay Christians. This is the experience of *enforced singleness.* A friend in his late twenties reports:

> I speak from the experience of the gay and lesbian community. We are the only group who are compelled to stay single. The legal system insists that we can't marry. The church insists that we remain celibate. There is no "option to marry" for us; so there is no real "choice" to remain single.

The prevailing norms in many societies and most religious groups continue to define homosexual adults as necessarily single. Because their sexual orientation is seen as a threat, they are encouraged to remain separate, isolated, uncommunicative. Their sexual inclinations, even if not sinful, are still judged unnatural and unworthy. However, a strong indication of adult maturity is a growing comfort with one's identity and lifestyle. If, as is often the case for lesbians and gay men, singleness is made to feel like a quarantine, psychological and religious maturing will be impaired. By enforcing singleness, society and the church suggest that commitment and fidelity are unachievable for gays and lesbians. To contest this punitive singleness, some people are tempted to act out an erratic or compulsive sexual style. But this just defeats hopes for genuine intimacy. Society's prejudice becomes a self-fulfilling prophecy: the homosexual person is left not only single but alone.

When homosexual Christians do attempt to forge a lasting union, both church and society resist acknowledgment. A lesbian couple who have lived in a committed, faithful union for seven years must present themselves in the larger community as two single women who just happen to share a house. Two men whose life together is a major source of their creativity find that being known as a gay couple is too risky.

Pressures from within and from without may push a homosexual Christian toward a heterosexual marriage. Against such pressures, the gay or lesbian Christian tries to discern a sense of vocation and identity and asks, "What kind of intimacy and lifestyle fit who I am and how God has gifted me?" For the lesbian or gay or bisexual Christian—as for the heterosexual—the challenge of intimacy begins in the invitation to come to know and then to love and trust who we are. Our ability to be faithful to who we are—and this includes our sexual identity—grounds our ability to be faithful to other people and to values.

Vocation: The Choice to Be Single

Getting married is no longer an automatic sign in U.S. culture that a person is fully adult. As delaying marriage until the thirties or later becomes a more acceptable option, young people also find greater freedom to choose a single life. A colleague in her mid-thirties reports:

> I've not determined that I will not get married, but I can't operate with the sense that I'm "waiting." I can't put off other decisions about myself and my life because I'm waiting to get married.

As young adults shape their lives through commitment to work and friendship, some find that marriage will probably not be part of their future. Does a person *choose* to remain single, or is this something that just happens? The answer to this question is different for each person, but the comment of a colleague in his forties seems representative of many:

> I did not really start out with a choice to be single or not to marry. I made decisions about my life and my work as choices came up, and these have given shape and direction to my life. One of the results of these decisions is that I am not married.

For many people, then, being single is not a direct or explicit choice. Nor does one's life as single happen only by default—because "Prince Charming" or "the girl of my dreams" did not show up. In reality, a subtler evolution guides the maturing of many single adults.

Single adults often express a special affirmation of this lifestyle in their forties. They come to the point where they can say, "This is who I am. I recognize and accept that I am unlikely to marry. This feels good and right for me." With such an affirmation, single adults can let go of the family and cultural pressures that may still haunt them. They can turn away from a lingering sense of self as "still not married."

In both theology and spirituality, the Catholic understanding of vocation has been undergoing a dramatic transformation. Christian vocation is both an invitation from God and a response to this call. In an earlier piety, "to have a vocation" meant to be a vowed religious or a priest. The rest of us, married or single, had to muddle along without any special religious identity or sense of calling. Today a more adequate theology of baptism recognizes that every Christian has a vocation—a personal invitation to live one's life transformed by grace.

Our vocation, which expresses our Christian identity, is an invitation to live a life shaped by two powerful influences: the values of faith and the qualities—strengths and limits—we find in our self. Grounded in the gifts and inclinations we discover in our self, our religious identity becomes real in particular choices. We must discern how *we* will love our neighbor, care for the world, witness to justice and mercy. Through these acts of our vocation, we are revealed to our self.

Gradually, Christians are coming to a more fruitful distinction of *vocation* and *lifestyle*. A vocation refers to that profound and continuing call that each of us, with effort, can discern. God invites us to give our life's energy to *this* way of loving and working and contributing to the world. A vocation, like a dream or life-ambition, is our deepest and best hope for our life. Our dream may be very clear (to be an architect or a marine biologist or a police officer) or remain somewhat vague (to help kids in trouble or to make the world a better place). But it moves us to become our best self. As Christians we recognize that this dream, our vocation, comes as gift; it is part of God's hope for our life. This holy ambition runs deeper than any particular job; it survives the detours and failures that are part of any journey of faith.

On the other hand, our lifestyle points to the patterns we develop as we attempt to live out our vocation. Our lifestyle includes the value commitments that guide our decisions, the choices we make about friends and work and leisure, the way we organize our time. Whatever our vocation, we must each determine the lifestyle that best supports this calling. For many single Christians, broadening of the idea of vocation and distinguishing it from lifestyle come as a gift. This insight encourages singles to explore and trust their emerging vocation, whatever it is. They are also invited to examine how being single will be part of their unique vocation. Their vocation is not "to be single." Their vocation—like that of celibate or married Christians—is the larger plot and purpose of their life, through which God gradually reveals them to themselves. Being single—whether for a time or for one's life, by choice or by circumstances—is part of that larger movement of grace, but seldom the defining characteristic of one's identity or vocation.

Vocation and Fidelity

Beneath our social roles and beyond all social expectations, we seek to discern and follow our vocation. Revealed to us through our relationships and our action in the world, this vocation is personal but not private. Fidelity challenges us to be faithful to the unfolding story of our own life with God. In a culture like ours—which insists on marriage as *the* adult lifestyle—some Christians find that fidelity to their own vocation does not include marriage. Thus, a young man or woman in the late thirties begins to suspect that marriage will not be a part of his or her life. This can be disappointing or confusing. A woman may ask, "Should I marry, even if this means going against my best judgment?" A man may scrutinize his motives and wonder, "Am I just being selfish? Am I afraid to make a commitment?" The challenge here is to discover and accept who we are becoming and the direction that seems most genuine for our life.

Fidelity is—like identity—a question of congruence, of fit between who we are and how we live. Fidelity is also related to confidence—having faith in ourself. Coming gradually to a clearer sense of vocation—what we can and should do with our life—we learn to trust ourself. Trusting ourself and believing in the direction of our life, we gain confidence to meet the surprises and changes that life still has in store.

Self-confidence, as an important part of the strength of fidelity, is also related to conscience. Conscience—the ability to discern and decide what is right—is grounded in a sense of who we are and what we are for. A well-developed conscience allows us to trust our decisions. Our choices and actions are *conscientious* because they fit our commitments and flow from our values; they are faithful to who we are as *this Christian adult.* Conscience allows us to make choices about our lifestyle, not out of a compulsive *should* nor mainly to please others, but in fidelity to our deepening sense of vocation.

Our vocation is not a single call given once at the beginning of adult life. We hear God's invitation repeatedly in the various challenges and crises of our life. Thus our vocation becomes a lifelong conversation with God. Fidelity is not simply an act of clinging to the past. Fidelity means staying in the conversation.

Over the course of our life we may expect to hear new invitations and face unexpected demands. Fidelity provides resilience and courage in responding to where life leads us. Unforeseen changes in ourselves and others—whether new discoveries or failures—impel us to revise, deepen, or alter our commitments. Then we are drawn into the mystery of a life still being revealed to us, a life we do not fully control. A friend in his forties sums up his sense of discovery by saying:

> There is a mystery in my life. For a long time I've wanted to be married and I still have a sense that I'll marry some day. But I realize now there is a mystery in life. It may be that I won't marry. I don't know what the unfolding may be. I think I will welcome however my life goes. But the problem comes in the anxiety I pick up in our society. I feel good about myself, but I feel strangely "incomplete" in terms of the subtle norms I know are operative—at work, among my family members, even among some of my friends.

Single Christians face a special challenge in separating the cultural messages about the superiority of marriage from the deeper intimations, given in grace, that guide their integrity. Supported by fidelity, their vocation and lifestyle come together in choices that are both satisfying and fruitful. Beyond this, their lives become a gift to the church, signs of the diversity of God's design for generous love.

REFLECTIVE EXERCISE

List the single people who are part of your own life these days—family members, friends and co-workers, perhaps yourself as well. Drawing on your experience of their lives, consider these questions.

As you see it, what are some of the benefits of being single? What do you find attractive or satisfying or admirable?

From your perspective, what are some of the burdens of being single? What strikes you as troublesome or difficult or undesirable?

Where do the single people you know best find support for their lifestyle and vocation?

Is the church part of the lives of single people you know? If so, what shape does this participation take?

ADDITIONAL RESOURCES

Throughout his helpful discussion in *Loving Relationships,* Robert Shelton takes up explicitly the experience of those who are not married. Margaret Farley provides trustworthy guidance for singles and others in *Personal Commitments: Beginning, Keeping, Changing* and in her more recent book *Just Love.* In *Singles at the Crossroads,* Albert Hsu offers biblical and theological perspectives and seasoned advice for single persons. In *Living Alone,* pastoral counselors Herbert Anderson and Freda Gardner respond to the experiences of single people across the lifespan.

Psychologists Marc St. Camille and Lou Moretti discuss the lives of single persons in practical and affirming ways in *It's Okay to Be Single;* see also Marjorie Barton, *Living Single in a Double World.* Grace Baruch, Rosalind Barnett, and Caryl Rivers report the findings of their research into the lives of women approaching midlife in *Life Prints.* In *Single Again: A Guide for Women Starting Over,* Victoria Jaycox draws sympathetically on the experience of women who are "suddenly single" through divorce or widowhood, to offer support and practical advice for others who face these challenging circumstances.

Karen Lebacqz suggests a fresh starting point for the discussion of sexual morality in "Appropriate Vulnerability: A Sexual Ethic for Singles"; see also *Sexual Diversity and Catholicism,* edited by Patricia Beattie Jung with Joseph Coray and Jean Sheridan's *The Unwilling Celibate: A Spirituality for Single Adults.*

Stephanie Dowrick discusses the connections between loneliness and identity in *Intimacy and Solitude: Balancing Closeness and Independence.* In *The Stations of Solitude,* Alice Koller explores her personal experience of being alone as its ripens into the resource of solitude. In *Seasons of Strength,* we examine the crises and invitations through which a Christian vocation unfolds; see also our discussion there of "The Virtue of Self-Intimacy."

7

Christian and Homosexual: The Paths of Love

LET US START WITH A PERSONAL STATEMENT. Thirty years ago we began both our shared journey of marriage and our shared career as ministry educators. Then—as now—we were committed Catholics and serious students of human nature. And we were also seriously shortsighted. Oblivious of the experience of friends and colleagues with whom we shared life every day, we knew (so we thought) no homosexual Christians.

In our first summer of teaching, a student in one of our graduate courses came to our office to talk with us both. In his early thirties, Gary was already established in his teaching career and now working toward an advanced degree. But what Gary wanted to speak with us about was not our academic lectures; he wanted to tell us he was falling in love. But there was more to it; he was falling in love with another man.

This initial conversation lasted several hours, and further discussions with Gary continued over the summer. We looked together at many sides of the homosexuality debate—theology and psychology, faith and morals, nature and nurture. And over the course of these conversations we became friends. One of the early and enduring gifts of Gary's friendship came on that first afternoon as he told us the story of his new relationship. The surprising attraction when they first met, the exhilarating delight of spending time together, the hope this relationship promised for the future—these were experiences we too had known in the months leading to our own marriage. His story was not about promiscuity or sordid sexual compulsion. Gary was giving an

account of one of God's great gifts—the miracle and mystery of finding someone to love.

In the course of this conversation and the ones that followed over
the years with many other friends and colleagues, we have been moved
by a conversion of heart. What if homosexuals are not "them," dangerously different people whose lives are consumed in deviant behavior? What if the truth is much simpler and more significant: we are the
body of Christ and part of our body is lesbian and gay.

Who are the homosexual members of the body of Christ? They are
our siblings and our children, our friends and fellow parishioners.
These are persons like us, striving to live generous lives of maturing
faith. As we speak the truth to one another, we recognize that, in our
sexuality as in so much else, we are more alike than we are different.
This realization marked the beginning of our conversion.

Learning from the Faithful

The change of heart we experienced is happening many places
throughout the community of faith. In prayer groups and ministry
networks, in parish communities and other small group settings, people of faith gather in practical and profound ways. We touch lives so
different from our own but, in their fragility and quiet courage, so
similar. As Christians speak honestly with one another about our life
and our hopes, about our longing for love, we recognize a common
passion.

Arousal is the wellspring of sexuality for all of us—whether heterosexual or homosexual. And for all of us these inclinations are filled
with both promise and peril. For gay and straight persons alike, our
passions are subject to every manner of distortion, as the human history of selfishness and sexual violence attests. For all of us, questions
remain of how we will express our affection and how we might transform emotional attraction into enduring commitment. And we each
face the challenge of finding a lifestyle and forging fidelities that are
both adult and Christian.

Understanding Homosexuality

A small but significant percentage of the human community is drawn
emotionally and physically to persons of the same gender. Researchers

estimate the number ranges between four percent and ten percent of the adult population. By whatever count, the number of people who discover themselves sexually attracted to members of the same gender is substantial.

This attraction, or sexual orientation, is not a matter of choice; it does not result from a personal decision. A man who comes to recognize that he is gay, for example, does not *choose* to set aside his "natural and normal" attraction to women so that he can experience a more perverse kind of sexual excitement. A woman who discovers she is a lesbian does not *choose* to feel an "unnatural" delight in the presence of another woman; for her, this is the most natural feeling imaginable! Sexual orientation—this abiding disposition of mind and heart and body—is, in the words of Episcopal bishop Bennet Sims, a "bestowed identity." The bishop's phrase suggests that a homosexual orientation is not a curse but a gift. Although one's sexual orientation is not chosen, it is, of course, a responsibility. Both gay and straight Christians bear the responsibility to love in ways that make their lives fruitful.

Theologian Jack Bonsor reminds us that "sexual orientation embraces more than the object of erotic passion. It involves our desire for the goods of intimacy, friendship and romantic relationships." Psychologists suggest three indications of sexual orientation: persistent patterns of attraction, enduring experiences of emotional intimacy, and continuing manifestations of devoted love. These indications work for heterosexual orientation and homosexual orientation alike. A person who experiences "persistent patterns of attraction, enduring experiences of emotional intimacy, and continuing manifestations of devoted love" toward others of the same gender is recognized as constitutively homosexual.

Reliable evidence of one's sexual orientation develops slowly and is seldom fully available before late adolescence. It is gradually, then, that we come to recognize our sexual identity. But since most societies expect and reward only heterosexual behavior, people who fit this expectation usually pay little attention to defining their sexual orientation. But for young people who discover their homosexual orientation, the process of discovery is often surrounded by secrecy and shame.

Why are some of us homosexual? Neither psychology nor medical science has yet a satisfactory answer to that question. But we do know that homosexual orientation does not arise from faulty parenting, as the older Freudian stereotype of the distant father and the smothering mother would hold. We also know that homosexual orientation is no longer judged to be a psychological disorder; in 1973, based on compelling research findings, the American Psychiatric Association removed homosexuality from its list of mental disorders and in 1975 the American Psychological Association followed suit.

In addition, we know that constitutive homosexual orientation is seldom amenable to change. Neither shock therapy nor pastoral counseling succeeds in altering this essential component of personal identity. The challenge in ministry is not to turn homosexual Christians into heterosexuals, but to support one another in learning to love faithfully and well.

The enduring sense of sexual orientation that we know as constitutive homosexuality differs from a more transient same-sex attraction. A student in a women's boarding school may feel strongly attracted to another student or to a woman teacher. Or a young man in the male-only environment of a seminary feels sexually aroused by another student or a professor. Spending long months in a single-sex environment, some people experience the stirring of sexual attraction for members of the same sex. This should not be surprising. As humans, we are designed to share affection, care, and concern. If our only companions are members of the same sex, these may well be the persons for whom we experience affective longings. Many people who have this experience find that, upon leaving the same-sex environment, their attraction to members of the same sex subsides.

An extreme and tragic example of what might be called "situational homosexuality" comes from the prison system. Confined in a same-sex environment and deprived of genuine friendship and meaningful work, some inmates turn to promiscuous and violent sexual behavior to express their outrage. Such tragic activity is more a symptom of the dehumanizing atmosphere of the prison than a sign of sexual orientation.

Compassion and Conversation

The conversation about homosexuality must begin in our own communities of faith. The U.S. Catholic Bishops wisely recognized this imperative in "Always Our Children," their compassionate pastoral letter to parents and teachers. The letter begins with a plea to parents not to reject a daughter or son who is homosexual. These are still our children—"always our children"—and they are beloved of God. The pastoral letter reminds the Catholic community that a person's sexual orientation is a "deep-seated dimension of one's personality and (we should) recognize its relative stability." The bishops reaffirm that "sexual orientation is experienced as a given, not as something freely chosen." And since it is not chosen, a person's homosexual orientation cannot be seen as sinful. Finally, the bishops strongly encourage parents and pastors to "welcome homosexual persons into the faith community."

As more and more faith communities welcome their homosexual members, Christians come to know one another more deeply. For many heterosexual Christians, sharing the faith journey of a lesbian friend or gay colleague brings startling realizations. Compassion takes root as we learn each other's histories of grace and failure, of woundedness and healing. Similar stories emerge: the same excitement at the possibility of love and the same terror that devotion might not endure. New recognitions dawn: our communities include many homosexual couples who share lives of faithful and fruitful love. These couples, like the rest of us, know both the blessings and the challenges of commitment. Their relationships, like our own, are shaped by generosity and misunderstanding, by conflict and forgiveness. Sharing our stories, we discern more surely that sexuality and spirituality are not mutually exclusive concerns. Sexual longings and spiritual hopes share space in our heart.

Human sexuality is much more than a hormonal drive or a lust for genital expression. Our spontaneous impulses of desire and affection are the wellspring of human love. Moving us beyond self-centeredness, these arousals are more than "near occasions of sin." For many Christians, homosexual and heterosexual alike, it is in the life of intimacy we share with our sexual partner that the love of God becomes most real. We recognize that our sexuality is the very root of our vitality, the source of our fruitful engagement with life—through our children, to be sure, but also through the many bonds of affection that sustain our friendships and communities. Sexuality, our lives attest, is often an occasion of grace.

But a welcoming stance does not always characterize our faith communities. Lesbian and gay Catholics continue to be instructed in official church documents that—in them—erotic arousal is disordered. Quite apart from responsible decisions about expression and abstinence (decisions that confront us all), the inclinations of their hearts are judged to be depraved. Their arousals, we are told, do not and cannot resonate with the delight in God's creation.

As a result, many churches adopt a "don't ask, don't tell" policy, not unlike that of the U.S. military. Lesbian and gay members are tolerated if they maintain a low profile, discussing their sexual orientation only in the privacy of the counseling session or the confessional, while remaining silent in public. The conventional advice offered to heterosexual Christians here is to "hate the sin and love the sinner." Tolerant as this may sound, it seems not to work. In real life, our responses do not divide so neatly. Loving respect for other persons proves difficult when we designate their sexuality as disordered.

Society's Options: Closet or Rebel

Today Christians who are homosexual embrace many lifestyles: some choose the spiritual disciplines of sexual abstinence; others are abstinent by circumstance more than by choice. Many lesbians and gay men find that their faith journey includes the blessings of devoted sexual love; still others pray for the gift of genuine intimacy, even as they acknowledge this absence in their life now.

But until recently in U.S. society, many gays and lesbians felt that they faced only two options: to remain hidden in the closet or to "come out" in some dramatic way. The closeted experience of secrecy and shame promised refuge, but at a severe cost: a continuing friction of deception and denial that erodes personal integrity. Reacting against this intolerable strain, some moved to the opposite extreme, embracing a spontaneous—even promiscuous—celebration of sexuality. The extravagant lives of artists and celebrities—Oscar Wilde, Gertrude Stein, Michel Foucault—stand as models for this "liberated" gay identity. And the media's accounts of gay bars and public baths, of fabulous costumes and flamboyant behavior, reinforced in wider society this image of the homosexual as social rebel.

The beginning of a new century brings greater perspective on these dire options. A closet is where we keep things out of sight. But inside the closet, clear vision is difficult and effective communication almost impossible. This protective space serves well as a hiding place, but not as a healthy place to live. In its dark confines, people neither grow nor flourish. For the individual lesbian or gay Christian, a closeted life may be safe—even by some definitions "chaste"—but it is seldom joyful or generous. And when devoted gay and lesbian couples must remain anonymous in our churches, the whole community suffers. Deprived of this practical witness of faithful love, a faith community may have only society's inherited prejudices to guide its understanding of homosexuality.

The role of rebel, too, has severe limitations. Embracing the public role of rebel generates an exhilarating sense of personal freedom. But this heady mood is quickly replaced by the awareness that this sub-culture has its own demands. As in any group, there are both explicit expectations and unspoken codes of conduct. Conforming to the "out-law" role initially provides release from the bigotry of the surround-ing culture, but ultimately reinforces social isolation.

In a welcoming community of faith, the gay and lesbian Christian finds support for another way of living. Beyond the dark confines of the closet and the flamboyance of the rebel, the good news invites us—homosexual and heterosexual alike—into commitments of generous and responsible love. As psychologist Sidney Callahan notes, the sex-ual behavior of homosexual Christians stands accountable to "the same moral conditions required of heterosexual marital activity, such as commitment, love and lifelong fidelity." All Christians are called to chastity. But the virtue of chastity is not the same as the charism of celibacy. For the vast majority of Christians, gay and straight, chastity describes the quality of our sexual loving, not a commitment of sex-ual abstinence.

The U.S. Catholic bishops have helped clarify this all-embracing nature of chastity. In their pastoral letter "Always Our Children," the bishops offer this definition: "chastity means integrating one's thoughts, feelings and actions in the area of human sexuality in a way that values and respects one's own dignity and that of others." For most gay and lesbian (as well as most heterosexual) Christians, this integration is pursued not in a celibate lifestyle but in a life that includes sexual love. The signs of the holiness of these relationships are the same for us all: faithfulness and fruitfulness over time. The *New Catholic Catechism* recognizes the uneven progress that marks—for us all—this integration of mature sexuality: "Chastity has *laws of growth* which progress through stages marked by imperfections and too often by sin" (#2343). Here too we are more alike than we are dif-ferent.

The Symbolic Life of Human Sexuality

The bishops' definition of chastity challenges an earlier tendency, in both religious documents and popular culture, to reduce human sexuality to biology—physical actions with reproductive potential. When sexuality is equated with sexual intercourse, it is a short step to judging that the significance of sexual sharing is found exclusively in the procreation of children. Movement beyond this reductionist view is well begun in our churches; no longer is Christianity's perspective rooted in Augustine's justification of marriage as a "remedy for concupiscence." This shift represents a richer appreciation of the symbolic life of sexuality.

Humans are meaning-makers. We invest our experience with significance. Sex becomes humanly significant through the meanings we find in this basic human activity. As we saw in Chapter 3, sexuality is shaped by the meanings our culture assigns—to our bodies, our affections, our gender differences.

Understanding how sex is symbolic may be easier if we start with a look at another basic human activity—eating. Humans must eat to survive; this basic need influences us every day of our lives. Without careful attention to this part of our life, we simply perish.

But among humans, eating is about much more than consuming sufficient nutrients. Eating is a source of pleasure. The delights of taste and aroma quicken our appetite for food, for life. The pleasure of eating recruits us to the business of survival, and we quickly realize that the pleasure of food reaches beyond the private satisfaction of a basic instinct. The symbolic life of eating extends to the sense of communion we associate with food. Humans prefer to eat together. Sharing our food, though not absolutely necessary, enriches the satisfaction available to us all.

The activity of eating is taken up symbolically into a family's and community's broader experience of sustenance; being together at table we are nourished in ways that reach beyond the calories. For Christians the action of eating is folded into the symbolic experience of Eucharist. We break bread together in a grateful gathering, in remembrance of Jesus' action and as recommitment to our common life in Christ. Physical eating and spiritual nourishment embrace.

The symbolic life of food includes the rhythm of feast and fast. On special occasions, humans gather to celebrate with food. Our feasting honors both survival and bounty. Here we do not merely consume the necessary food groups; we show off! Special foods are prepared, perhaps some wine is shared. We bring out dishes and cups reserved for just such occasions; we adorn the table with special coverings and set out flowers and candles. With these "unnecessary" necessities we acknowledge that the human spirit needs to splurge. Jews and Christians recognize the feast as a sign of God's own lavishness. "On this mountain for all peoples, Yahweh Sabaoth is preparing a banquet of rich food, a feast of fine wines, of succulent food and fine wines" (Isaiah 25:6). And in many religious traditions, the feast is a gracious act of inclusion. All are invited to the table. We learn again that the genuine feast is a communal art, not a private indulgence.

Religious traditions across the world recommend fasting as companion to the feast. At its best, the motive that guides fasting is not hatred of the body. Instead, we interrupt our ordinary patterns of eating so that we might be attentive to other hungers. In the emptiness of the fast, we try to attune ourselves to more subtle soundings of the spirit, to desires and needs that are easily lost in the regular routines of our lives. Fasting, whether from food or conversation or sexual sharing, is often the *no* we choose, in order to protect the *yes* of our deeper commitments.

For humans, sex too has a symbolic life. Without offspring, our species will surely perish. But because we are humans, this essential energy of reproduction assumes multiple meanings and shapes many forms of fruitfulness. Sex is part of procreation and also part of pleasure. Early in our lives we may assume its pleasure is just for ourselves. But the gift of another's love awakens us to a deeper joy: sharing pleasure. In sexual sharing shaped by love and respect, the physical union can become sacramental—effecting the communion it symbolizes. Christians know this experience as grace.

Maturity brings the rhythm of feasting and fasting to lives of committed love, homosexual and heterosexual. At times we feast, delighting in the passion that unites us and even sometimes, as in the biblical *Song of Songs,* celebrating our delight as a reminder of God's lavish love. We learn the disciplines that accompany the sexual feast: attentiveness to our partner and a mutual responsibility for our lovemaking and its life consequences. And at times we fast, particularly when our partner is ill or absent. We learn to say no to other relationships, even in the allure of sexual attraction, to protect the yes of our committed love. Our religious tradition attunes us even to those fasts that we do not choose; in the painful absence of a lover, we pray with Psalm 63: "my body aches for you like a dry and weary land."

The symbolic power of food and sex extends beyond these life-affirming instances. Addiction too is symbolic activity. Afflicted by shame or suffering, humans sometimes turn to food or drink or drugs to numb the pain. Addiction becomes the compulsive activity by which we distract ourselves from an intolerable part of our life. Addiction is, finally, not about satisfying some basic appetite—whether hunger or sexual desire. St. Augustine, who knew addiction in his own life, described its power as the yearning to "satisfy the insatiable." Addiction is not even about pleasure; addicts are not enjoying their lives. Addiction's goal is absence; to distract ourselves—even if only briefly—from pain. Whether the addiction is to alcohol or gambling or shopping, these are but means for absenting ourselves from some intolerable part of our life.

And so it is with sexual addiction. Afflicted with an unbearable distress, we sometimes turn to the brief but powerful surge of sexual arousal—in pornography or promiscuity—to distract us from the pain. This sexual addiction—like alcohol addiction—is not primarily about experiencing pleasure. The intent is to flee from some part of personal experience that cannot be embraced. With its compulsive swing between excess and remorse, addiction performs a painful parody of the rhythm of feasting and fasting. As our society attests so clearly, this is an affliction that besets both heterosexuals and homosexuals.

While married Christians mature in the disciplined rhythm of feasting and fasting through their lives of sexual commitment, gay Christians have been instructed that their sexual lives must be a fast without a feast. Burdened with a sexual orientation whose every stirring of delight and attraction is, they are told, "essentially self-indulgent," lesbians and gay men are counseled to live as celibates, even if they have no evidence of a calling to this way of life. Many Christian homosexuals testify to the crippling and unfruitful results of following these directives.

Andrew Sullivan, himself a gay Catholic, writes of his own efforts to keep his relationships superficial in an effort to "prevent passion from breaking out." Looking back on his strenuous, if failed, efforts to conform to the church's official instruction to gay Catholics, he muses that what resulted was "a theological austerity (that) became the essential complement to an emotional emptiness." Instead of a Christian life rooted in personal dignity and generosity, his life became, in his words, "a lie covered over by a career."

Sullivan goes on to describe his conversion and the gradual reclaiming of his dignity: he remembers the "exhilaration I felt as my sexuality began to be incorporated into my life, . . . a sense of being suffused at last with the possibility of being fully myself before those I loved and before God." With this realization, the feast returns to a life that had been starved by a ruinous fast.

Conclusion

To open the conversation with gay and lesbian members of our faith communities is perilous business. Long-held convictions may come under question. Some of our attitudes and practices may well be recognized as shaped more by social bias than by the following of Christ. Deeper insight into the demands of the gospel may arise, challenging the lifestyles of homosexual and heterosexual Christians alike. These conversations—even when undertaken with respect—promise to be disconcerting and disturbing to us all. But in a community that knows itself as *semper reformanda*—always in need of reform—this conversation in faith will be welcomed as a gift.

In this effort to understand more deeply the links between sexuality and human dignity, we can be guided by Jesus, who asked his own friends the hard question, "Who is my family?" (see Matthew 12:48; Mark 3:33). In a world that "knew" what family meant and where its boundaries were, Jesus questioned the rules of belonging. He insisted that the powerful sway of bloodlines cannot define belonging for those who live by faith. The boundaries of race and gender and sexual orientation, constructed and defended by every culture, come under question when we open ourselves to his question, Who is our family?

Christians will continue to disagree about many questions of human sexuality. But if our conversations in the community of faith can be guided by honesty and compassion, if we can avoid the traps of stereotypes and prejudice, we will find ways to stand together. In such risky but necessary conversations, God will show us who our family is and how we are to love in the image of Jesus Christ.

REFLECTIVE EXERCISE

What is your own experience of respectful and honest conversations about sexuality? About homosexuality? In what settings has this kind of discussion been welcomed? In what settings has it proved to be useful?

Who, among your own family and friends and co-workers, are homosexual? What have you learned—about sexuality, about love, about fidelity, about faith—from the gay people who are close to you? If you are lesbian or gay yourself, with whom in the community of faith have you been able to share this dimension of your life?

In your experience—whether homosexual or heterosexual—what is most challenging in a discussion about sexuality? What benefits, if any, have you experienced from discussions of sexuality in the context of faith?

ADDITIONAL RESOURCES

The 1998 statement of the U.S. Catholic Bishops, "Always Our Children: A Pastoral Message to Parents of Homosexual Children and Suggestions for Pastoral Ministers," is available from the United States Catholic Conference Publishing Office in Washington, D.C.; we quote from the text that appeared in *Origins,* July 2, 1998. The helpful footnotes in this document note the few but significant changes in the final draft of this letter. Robert Nugent and Jeannine Gramick provide a careful discussion of homosexuality within the guidelines of official Catholic teaching in their *Building Bridges: Gay and Lesbian Reality and the Catholic Church;* see also Gerald Coleman, *Homosexuality: Catholic Teaching and Pastoral Practice;* and Peter J. Liuzzi, *With Listening Hearts: Understanding the Voices of Lesbian and Gay Catholics.*

Among the many recent reflections on being Catholic and homosexual, see Mary Hunt, *A Fierce Tenderness: A Feminist Theology of Friendship;* John McNeill, *Both Feet Firmly Planted in Mid-Air: My Spiritual Journey;* Maurice Shinnick, *This Remarkable Gift: Being Gay and Catholic;* Eric Stoltz, "Notes from a Community—Catholic and Gay"; and Elizabeth Stuart, *Just Good Friends: Toward a Lesbian and Gay Theology of Relationships.* We quote Andrew Sullivan from his article

"Alone Again, Naturally"; see also his book *Love Undetectable: Notes on Friendship, Sex, and Survival.* For an insightful reflection from a Protestant and politically conservative perspective, see Bruce Bawer, *A Place at the Table.*

For comprehensive discussions of factors that contribute to and detract from psychological well-being and personal integrity among homosexual women and men, see *The Course of Gay and Lesbian Lives* by Bertram J. Cohler and Robert Galatzer-Levy, and *Lesbian, Gay, and Bisexual Identities over the Lifespan,* edited by Anthony D'Augelli and Charlotte Patterson. Bernadette Brooten offers a compelling historical analysis in *Love Between Women: Early Christian Responses to Female Homoeroticism.* In *Coming Out Within: Stages of Spiritual Awakening for Lesbians and Gay Men,* Craig O'Neill traces the connections between gay sexuality and spirituality. James Empereur provides theological insight and pastoral sensitivity in *Spiritual Direction and the Gay Person.*

Catholic psychologist Sidney Callahan's reflections appeared in her discussion "Why I Changed My Mind: Thinking about Gay Marriage." We also quote from theologian Jack Bonsor's discussion "Homosexual Orientation and Anthropology: Reflections on the Category 'Objective Disorder.'" Theologian Eileen Flynn provides persuasive reasons for opening the dialogue about homosexuality within the community of faith in "Responding to the 'Gay Agenda.'" Walter Wink brings together the work of several Christian theologians in *Homosexuality and Christian Faith: Questions of Conscience for the Church.* See also the significant collection of essays in *Sexual Diversity and Catholicism: Toward the Development of Moral Theology,* edited by Patricia Beattie Jung with Joseph A. Coray.

8

The Gift of Celibacy

C HRISTIAN FAITH PROCLAIMS ITS DEEPEST TRUTH in paradoxes. Like the grain of wheat, we must die in order to find life. We meet Christ in the unlikely guise of the sick and the imprisoned and the stranger. Celibacy is another of our faith's paradoxes. As Christians we know that we can love one another well apart from sexual sharing; we recognize that, even without offspring, we can live fruitful and generous lives. But in a culture such as ours, obsessed with sex as performance, this paradox provokes surprise and disbelief.

Celibacy is a durable mystery. From early on, some who follow Christ have chosen a path that excludes marriage and family. Over centuries of Christian history and across a wide range of cultural contexts, many people have experienced committed celibacy as a grace. This lifestyle has nurtured Christians in their personal journeys of faith. In addition, celibacy has borne fruit in generous service to the world as celibate women and men served in the formal ministry of the church.

A consideration of the lifestyle of vowed celibacy is essential in any discussion of Catholics and sexuality. As we turn to that consideration, let us offer an initial clarification. Although we—the authors—are married, the reality of committed celibacy is significant to us, personally and professionally. Our ministry puts us in touch with the convictions and concerns of many religious and priests; our friends who are vowed celibates share with us the wisdom of their own experience. So it is as interested and sympathetic companions that we observe the ongoing conversation about the meaning of celibacy for the church today.

In reevaluating the meaning of sexuality, the community of faith comes to reexamine the lifestyle of celibacy. In the process, some earlier understandings of celibacy have come under question. These images and expectations no longer provide celibate Christians with a compelling explanation for their own lives. They no longer provide the basis of a genuine appreciation of celibacy in the larger community of faith. Catholics today struggle to come to a renewed vision of celibacy as an authentic Christian way of life.

The vitality of the gift of celibacy has been repeatedly proven in its ability to take on new meaning, to be persuasive in many different historical and cultural settings. The challenge now is not to do away with celibacy but to find what meaning this gift holds for the future. Like other parts of Christian faith, celibacy will survive by being purified. Our goal in this chapter is to examine where we are, as a community of faith, in the conversation about the purpose and practice of celibacy today.

The Why of Celibacy

The why of celibacy raises questions of meaning and motive. What is the religious significance of the lifestyle of celibacy? Why do some Christians commit themselves to this way of following Jesus ? Among Catholics in the 1940s and 1950s, the religious meaning of celibacy was clear. The church recommended this special way of life to those who would follow the path of perfection. Celibacy, or consecrated chastity, was understood to be one of the *evangelical counsels.* It was evangelical because it was rooted in the gospel. It was a counsel or advice that Jesus issued to his followers. To the rich young man who inquired about holiness, Jesus replied: "If you would be perfect . . . leave all and follow me." In Catholic spirituality, the vowed life of poverty, chastity, and obedience came to be seen as the principal way in which this gospel call to perfection could be followed. Most Christians would seek God by the ordinary way of life and work in the world; consecrated celibacy was an option for those who would seek the "better way."

But why was the choice of celibacy a "better way"? In the piety that had come to prevail in Catholic life, virginity was seen as preferable to marriage. Both Mary and Jesus were virgins. Moreover, the choice of celibacy helped one avoid the snares of sexual engagement and the entanglements of human love. Many Christians had been taught that sex was inevitably involved in sin and that human love was a distraction from a wholehearted devotion to God. True, these suspicions were seldom stated so baldly, and our best theology constantly battled against these aberrations. But many of us who grew up Catholic were influenced by these powerful, even if unorthodox, sentiments.

The problem with linking the religious significance of celibacy to these convictions is, of course, that they are heretical. That is not what Christians believe. Some religious traditions *have* judged sex to be evil; Manicheism tempted the early Christians in this way. Christians, however, have consistently, even if not always successfully, insisted that sex—like all that God has created—is good.

Christians also dispute that the love of God is in competition with human love. In truth, some early proponents of an enforced celibacy for the clergy argued that the demands of marriage and family would distract the minister from his constant occupation with God. These advocates of celibacy were profoundly suspicious of the compatibility of the sacred and the sexual. But the best and most enduring conviction of Christians is that the love of God and the love of neighbor are essentially linked. In the love that others show us, we come to know the love of God. And only by loving other people is our love of God purified and matured.

The renewal of Catholic life generated by the Second Vatican Council brought with it a rethinking of the meaning of celibacy. The council's reaffirmation of the spirituality of marriage challenged earlier understandings of celibacy as the "better way" or "higher calling." Church historians showed that the lifestyle of vowed celibacy has emerged gradually, its meaning and purpose understood differently at different times in Christian tradition. Earlier explanations of celibacy no longer seemed adequate. Even when they were not in error, they could no longer persuade.

Over the past forty years the vocabulary of the evangelical counsels has undergone profound purification. Vowed religious do not live in poverty as much as they do in simplicity. Their shared responsibility in community life is better understood as mutual accountability than as obedience to a quasi-parental authority. And the chastity to which they aspire is not meant to deliver them from the dangerous demands of friendship, affection, and charity that other Christians face.

The spirituality of a "higher calling" drove a wedge in the community of faith, creating different classes of Christians. Recently this understanding has fallen into disuse. More and more celibates find that such a spirituality neither reflects their religious experience nor energizes their continuing commitment. An interpretation of celibacy as the "higher way" does not serve the rest of us either, since it no longer reveals to the larger community of faith the religious significance that celibacy can hold.

This leaves the Catholic community at a loss. Our understanding of celibacy is moving away from the image of the evangelical counsel, but as yet no well-developed or widely accepted interpretation of celibacy replaces this image. Such a new consensus is sure to emerge, but only as we listen to the living tradition of consecrated celibacy as it takes shape in our own time. In the meantime, we are all at a disadvantage. Here, as in so many other areas of sexuality, we sense that we know more than we are able to say. Our religious vocabulary has not kept pace with our religious experience. Fortunately, the images used today in the discussion of celibacy hint at an emerging theology.

We will examine three of these images that are used most often in theology and by celibate Catholics. In each image, we will point out the positive understanding of celibacy as well as some of its limitations. The images we will consider are celibacy as a charism, as a choice, and as a call.

Celibacy as a Charism

The image of celibacy as a charism is often part of current discussion. Sometimes the term is simply a rhetorical flourish, but often it has more substance. The intent here, as in the understanding of celibacy as an evangelical counsel, is to root the lifestyle of consecrated celibacy in the gospel. This is a fruitful direction for the discussion, since every Christian lifestyle finds its source and significance in the witness of Jesus the Christ. The understanding of celibacy as a charism will surely be strengthened if it can be shown to bear the marks of the other gospel charisms.

Recent biblical scholarship helps clarify the meaning of charism. St. Paul reported the charisms that enlivened the church in Corinth: preaching, healing, prophecy, administration. These vital activities in the early Christian communities had three essential characteristics. These were, first, *personal abilities*. Charisms are specific strengths, identifiable talents, activities that a particular member of the community does well.

Second, these abilities are experienced as *gifts*. A follower of Jesus who finds herself capable in these ways is drawn to acknowledge that more than just herself is involved. She readily admits, "This is something that I do well, but I am not the sole or even the principal author of this talent. I experience myself as gifted and I am grateful." These gifts, Paul reminds us, come from the Spirit (1 Corinthians 12:11). They are not the result of administrative decision or official largesse. Instead they are discovered throughout the community, due to the generosity of God's Spirit.

Third, genuine charisms serve a *distinctive purpose*. These talents are not for private satisfaction or personal aggrandizement but for the building up of the body of Christ. A charism is a gift that is meant to be given away. Acknowledged in gratitude, it is exercised in generosity. Charisms reside *in* particular persons but they exist *for* the community of faith.

If the image of charism is to serve as the basis for a more adequate appreciation of the religious significance of celibacy, then celibacy must be shown to meet these scriptural criteria. While celibacy is not listed among the charisms that Paul cites explicitly, that in itself is not the critical issue. Catholics are not biblical fundamentalists; our appreciation of God's action in human history is not limited to proof texts. But if the powerful scriptural category of charism is to be used to explore the meaning of celibacy in our own time, the lifestyle of consecrated celibacy will have to display the three characteristics of a charism. We will have to show how this way of living is rooted in personal ability, how it is experienced as a gift, and how it serves the larger needs and hopes of the community of faith. Many of us are confident that celibacy—at least in a purified form—can show these characteristics. But the Christian community needs to expand this discussion and make it available in a compelling way.

Celibacy as a Choice

Another image figures significantly in current theology and spirituality: celibacy as a *choice*. Here the discussion is especially sensitive to the negative attitudes toward sex that so easily creep into a piety of celibacy. Historically this piety had often urged Catholics to choose celibacy for negative reasons: to avoid the temptations of sex and the demands of a family. But, as Catholic theologians insist today, only if sex is evil, only if marriage is a "lesser way," is it praiseworthy to choose celibacy for these negative motives. The choice of celibacy must be a decision not *against*, but *for* something. The person must choose not just to avoid, but to engage. As with every Christian choice, the motivating force of this decision must be love for something. Christians make the decision to be celibate for the sake of the kingdom of God.

In some discussions celibacy is chosen for the sake of the eschatological kingdom, the reign of God at the end of history. Celibates live among us as witnesses to the end-time, "where there will be neither marriage nor giving in marriage." This perspective, which acknowledges the goodness of sex and significance of married love, reminds us that these are only limited and partial realities. At its best, human love reveals God's love for us. But the immediacy of sex and the complexity of our relationships often blind us to the larger transcendent presence of God who is love. The lifestyle of committed celibacy is chosen for the sake of the kingdom. The committed celibate serves humankind as a sign of contradiction, forcing us to confront the deeper issues of human existence and meaning that are so easily masked in our culture's obsession with sex.

This argument is not persuasive with everyone, but it has a powerful influence on many whose ministry brings them into contact with persons whose lives have been devastated by our culture's sexual compulsions. To know strong, mature, caring celibates is a liberating experience for those who have been sexually abused, for young people caught in prostitution, for people grown sated with sex and yet cynical of any other source of personal worth. The eschatological or symbolic value of celibacy in our sex-crazed culture is an area that deserves much more thought. But a theology of celibacy that focuses on its witness value also remains accountable to the important questions: Who is looking and what do they see?

The credibility of the Catholic Church in the area of sexuality is not unquestioned. Recent statements and actions make many persons of good will suspicious of what religious officials have to say on these issues. We must acknowledge that not many people today are looking to Catholic celibates for guidance and revelation concerning their sexuality. And some who do look at celibates do not see their lives as signs of love or generosity or joy. This theological interpretation of celibacy will become more credible as it confronts the practical question of what persons of good will see when they come in contact with the lives of religious celibates. Some suspect that many celibates are not faithful to their vows or that most are faithful only under duress and would marry if given that option. These perceptions undermine the persuasiveness of religious celibacy.

Another understanding of celibacy for the sake of the kingdom carries weight today. Participating in the mission of Jesus, some Christians are drawn into demanding work in potentially dangerous circumstances. They choose to share their life with the poor, care for the critically ill, work for social justice in the midst of politically repressive regimes. Devoting one's life to these efforts is often all-consuming; it can be perilous as well. Here the choice for celibacy may be part of a larger sense of vocation. A person reflects on the implications of his calling:

> Weighing the circumstances that surround my own life's work, I realize that wholehearted devotion to this mission will make it impossible—or at least difficult—for me to honor the practical and emotional commitments of marriage and family life. So, aware of the demands and dangers associated with my vocation, I've decided not to marry.

Celibacy is chosen not "for itself" but "for the sake of the kingdom."

This can be a compelling argument for committed celibacy. Some tasks in our time make these demands; some roles require such courage; some responsibilities ask for this kind of generous response. We have only to recall the patient heroism of the four women pastoral workers murdered in San Salvador or the witness of others who risk imprisonment and disgrace by speaking out for justice in the face of repression.

But we must acknowledge that most of us involved in the mission of Jesus are not engaged in this kind of difficult and dangerous work. Most persons who are celibate today are in fact involved in work that does not, on the face of it, exclude the commitments of marriage and family life. The experience of other Christian denominations shows us that effective religious leadership does not always require a celibate clergy. Protestant missionaries, usually married and often with families, have a long history of generous service in remote and dangerous settings. Within the Catholic community, more and more married persons are found in roles of pastoral ministry and religious leadership once available only to celibates. Catholics who are celibate, single, and married work side by side in ministry these days—doing similar work with similar results of success and failure. In this closer collaboration, many celibates recognize that in the lives of their lay colleagues the commitments of marriage and family life often do more to support effective ministry than to distract from it.

Another understanding of celibacy as a choice must be mentioned here. At issue is the linking of celibacy with priesthood. Scriptural studies have made clear that celibacy was not an essential element of Christian leadership in the New Testament: Simon Peter and others of Jesus' closest followers were clearly married; in the Pastoral Epistles bishops are described as married men (1 Timothy 3:2; 3:12; Titus 3:6). The study of Catholic history, however, shows the gradual development of the celibate priesthood: in the fourth century married priests were exhorted to abstain from sexual intercourse; gradually, fewer and fewer bishops and priests married; then in the twelfth century celibacy was made mandatory for priesthood in the Latin Rite. Because of this biblical and historical evidence, most theologians have concluded that celibacy is not a necessary part of the ministry of priesthood. Rather, celibacy is a religious discipline required by the Roman Catholic Church.

Compulsory celibacy is part of Catholic priesthood today. To be ordained, a candidate for priesthood must accept the requirement of celibacy. Seminarians know this from the outset; over the course of training they are made aware of the practical and spiritual requirements of the celibate way of life. Therefore, it is said, celibacy is a free choice made by those who are ordained.

Among many diocesan priests and seminarians, however, this discussion of celibacy as a choice rings hollow. Their experience is not that celibacy is a choice open to them in the Spirit. Rather it is a formal requirement demanded of them if they are to move forward toward ordination. For many, the choice they have made is for the ministry of community and liturgical leadership to which they know themselves to be called. In order to be allowed to exercise that ministry, they have accepted the stipulation that goes with it—that they will not marry. Many diocesan priests do not, in fact, experience celibacy as a personal charism or a vocational choice. They experience it neither as a gift of the Spirit nor as a personal strength. They would choose to marry if that were possible. Since marriage is not an option at this time, these priests strive courageously to live in a way that is faithful to their public declaration of celibacy, even though their own spiritual gifts and personal temperament do not offer them much support for this lifestyle.

Celibacy as a Call

We have been exploring the images that are part of the discussion of celibacy today. For many people, the most important image is celibacy as a call. The strength of this understanding of celibacy is its close connection with spirituality: celibacy is experienced as an integral part of one's personal journey of faith. This can be the experience of the young adult who feels drawn into a deepening relationship with the person of Jesus. Through prayer and discernment, often assisted by a spiritual director or other religious guide, she comes to recognize that her own spiritual journey includes remaining celibate. For her, celibacy is part of God's call. Here the decision for celibacy is rooted in an openness to God's mysterious action in one's own life.

For another person, the decision for celibacy is part of a call to live in religious community. He feels drawn to share life with this religious congregation. Their vision and values, their mission and spirit, the work they do, the way they live together appeal very strongly to him. After a period of reflection and evaluation, he comes to the conviction that this way of life can be for him a way to God. His commitment to celibacy is made as part of a larger commitment to share life with this particular religious group. Here again, celibacy is seen as part of one's personal journey of faith. The decision to remain celibate is made because it is seen as part of God's call *for this person* rather than because celibacy is objectively a higher or more holy way to live.

The mature witness of celibate persons in mid-life and beyond offers us another rich experience of celibacy as a personal call. This experience is an especially significant source of renewed appreciation of the meaning of celibacy today. These people have lived the celibate life for many years. Their experience bridges the gap between the earlier understanding of celibacy as the "higher calling" and the current confusion over the validity of the life choice of celibacy. Such mature members of the community of faith bring both candor and confidence to the discussion.

In moments of reflection, the mid-life religious muses:

The reasons that brought me to religious life are not the reasons that see me through today. My understanding of myself, my sexuality, what celibacy means, what it demands—all these have changed significantly. I am aware of the mixed motives that were part of my earliest decision for celibacy: generosity and fear, guilt and idealism, openness to God and susceptibility to social pressure. However, this hodgepodge of motives does not mean I made the wrong choice. I am aware that all important life choices combine a range of motives. But I also recognize that I have been able to face some of the shadows, to purify some of the compulsions that made my earlier decisions less than free. The convictions that hold me in this lifestyle today are in many ways different from the beliefs I held twenty years ago. But I remain celibate, or better, I continue to choose celibacy because it fits. As a celibate, I have grown and deepened and learned to love. The celibate life, with its joy and sorrow, has given me much of what is best in myself. This is the way I have been led; this has been the path of my own journey with God.

Mature celibates like this testify most convincingly to the adequacy of the celibate commitment today. The church in the United States is blessed with thousands of such mature religious and priests whose lives attest to the contemporary significance of celibacy. This is a rich source of information to bring more explicitly into the larger ecclesial discussion of celibacy. Such lives serve not as justifications of a questionable theology of the "higher way," but as witness to the power and purpose of celibacy as one of the trustworthy ways in which the Christian journey may be followed in faith.

Two Challenges

Christians continue to acknowledge that celibacy is an authentic way to live our religious faith. In the community of faith today we recognize how fruitful this paradoxical lifestyle can be. However, two special challenges for the survival of celibacy arise from our shared history.

The first challenge we face is to unyoke the gift of celibacy from biases against sexuality. Celibacy first flowered in a milieu hostile to sexuality and the body. Virginity was judged to be the most genuine way to live the faith. Marriage was a poor second best—a concession to nature and a sure distraction from Christian virtue.

Because sexual activity was portrayed as unavoidably stained by selfishness and compulsion, many Christians were attracted to the choice for a celibate life. As the bias against sex is healed, the negative motive for celibacy is removed. Increasingly Christians choose a celibate life, not to avoid the threat of sexuality but because consecrated celibacy fits their temperament, vocation, and spirituality. This lifestyle allows them to love generously and well.

The second challenge we face is to disengage the lifestyle of celibacy from the ministry of priesthood. Many Catholics remain unaware that the links between celibacy and priesthood were forged only gradually, in a historical process that began many years after the life of Jesus. In the fourth century, when the pastoral discipline of celibacy was first applied to priests who were not also monks, many priests and bishops were actually married. Not until almost eight hundred years later, in the Second Lateran Council of 1139, did the requirement of priestly celibacy become part of official church law.

Historical research shows that the growing conviction that priests ought not marry was strongly influenced by negative attitudes toward sexuality that dominated the Mediterranean world. These attitudes no longer prevail. Only slowly and painfully are we returning today to a more biblically based confidence in the compatibility of sexuality and spirituality.

The time has come for Catholics to disengage the choice for celibacy from the community service of the priestly ministry. Both celibacy and the priesthood will survive this separation. The ministry of the priesthood will profit by the influx of generous and gifted married persons, and celibacy will be appreciated as the special gift it is meant to be. This paradoxical grace will be a more convincing witness in those Christians who freely and courageously choose to follow the Lord in this way.

REFLECTIVE EXERCISE

Consider your own experience of committed celibacy. First, take a moment to recall a celibate person who has influenced you—a teacher or a pastor, perhaps a member of your own family or a close friend. What do you find most attractive or admirable about this person? In what ways has this person been influential in your life? What is the chief conviction about celibacy that you draw from this person's life?

Next, broaden the focus of your reflection by responding to these questions. What contribution does the Christian vision of celibacy make to you personally? As you see it, what contribution does the lifestyle of consecrated celibacy make to the community of faith? To the larger human community?

Finally, are there any concerns you have about the vision and lifestyle of celibacy in the Catholic community today?

ADDITIONAL RESOURCES

The work of theologian Sandra Schneiders continues to illumine the lived reality and theological significance of religious life; see *Finding the Treasure: Locating Catholic Religious Life in a New Ecclesial and Cultural Context.* Her discussion of celibacy is found in *Selling All: Commitment, Consecrated Celibacy and Community in Catholic Religious Life.* Sean Sammon's *An Undivided Heart: Making Sense of Celibate Chastity* offers an informed and honest look at the experience of consecrated celibacy today. Barbara Fiand's *Refocusing the Vision: Religious Life into the Future* examines the transformations facing religious life today. In *Poverty, Celibacy, and Obedience: A Radical Option for Life,* Diarmuid O'Murchu explores the positive dimensions of human consciousness that these religious vows both express and safeguard.

After Vatican II, a renewed dialogue about the meaning of celibacy sprang up in the church. Donald Goergan's classic treatise on sexuality and celibacy, *The Sexual Celibate,* was followed by Philip Keane's discussion of celibacy in his *Sexual Morality.* This dialogue continues today in Joan Chittister, *The Fire in These Ashes;* Michael Crosby, *Celibacy: Means of Control or Mandate of the Heart?;* Donald Cozzens, *The Changing Face of the Priesthood;* Richard Sipe, *Celibacy: A Way of Loving, Living, and Serving;* and Heinz Vogels, *Celibacy: Gift or Law.* See also the issue devoted to celibacy that appeared as a supplement to the Jesuit spirituality journal *The Way.*

Edward Schillebeeckx traces the appearance of celibacy as a requirement for priesthood in his book *Ministry.* Jo Ann McNamara examines the early history of consecrated celibacy among women in *A New Song: Celibate Women in the First Three Christian Centuries.*

Part Three

The Conversation Continues

T HE ONGOING MYSTERY OF OUR SEXUAL LIVES brings us to questions of gender. How shall we be together—as women and men, as friends and lovers—in fruitful and enduring ways? Part 3 begins in conversation about our differences as women and men. Next we examine evolving understandings of what gender requires: what it means to be feminine; what masculinity entails. Finally, we track the contemporary discussion of sexual self-pleasuring in both moral theology and psychological research.

9

Women and Men:
What Difference Do Our
Differences Make?

A MAN. A WOMAN. What could be simpler, more natural? Two obviously different yet complementary versions of humanity. But why, then, the confusion and conflict between women and men today? Why feminism? Why a men's movement? Why such discord and disagreement about the role of women in society and in the church?

Science tells us that women and men differ in only three percent of our common DNA inheritance as *homo sapiens,* but this scant variation appears in every cell. Under the lens of human culture, this minimal—and critical—difference magnifies into the realm of gender. In this chapter we will examine how gender affects our relationships of love and work.

Looking at Gender Differences

We note three approaches to the study of gender today. Many studies emphasize the differences between men and women; some downplay these differences, others reexamine the social consequences of "difference" itself.

Emphasizing the Differences

This approach sees women and men embodying different capabilities. Sometimes these differences are understood to be genetically based and linked to the evolutionary success of the human species. Lists of masculine and feminine traits differ from study to study, but gender-specific abilities are usually presented as opposites. Some familiar examples of this masculine/feminine polarity include:

thinking/feeling

achieving/nurturing

doing/being

working/loving

Characteristically, these gender-linked abilities are understood as mutually exclusive. Sometimes a stark dichotomy is implied: a person may excel in *either* work *or* love, but not both. Sometimes the traits are placed at opposite ends of a continuum: being *more* capable of supporting the development of other people means being *less* capable of personal achievement. But in either model, "you can't have it both ways." So, in this view, a man will jeopardize his rational decision-making ability (masculine trait) if he gives too much attention to how people will be affected (feminine trait); a woman is unlikely to succeed in using her collaborative skills (feminine trait) in her exercise of effective leadership (masculine trait).

Downplaying the Differences

Some studies downplay gender differences by accepting findings drawn from research on men as also describing women. Investigations such as this—once common in medical research—include only men in their analysis but then apply their findings to everyone. In theory, this approach implies that gender is not a significant factor in health or human behavior. In practice, earlier researchers seldom reflected on these underlying assumptions. They simply accepted men's experience as "normal" and measured women's experience against that norm. If studies of women produced different findings, these differences were usually interpreted as deficiencies.

A more thoughtful resistance to seeing women and men as different is frequently raised by other social scientists. On many tests, gender differences appear when the scores of all women are averaged and then compared with the average scores of all men. But comparing average scores in this way (*between* men-as-a-group and women-as-a-group) masks the real diversity that exists in human experience. In virtually every study, the differences found *among* women (and, likewise, *among* men) turn out to be greater than the average difference *between* women and men. For example, small differences are regularly found between average math test scores of men and women. But these same tests show a wide range of difference among the men themselves, as there is among women.

Exploring the Social Consequences
of Gender Difference

Studies here begin by acknowledging that the most enduring differences between women and men—whether measured across historical periods or across contemporary cultures—are inequalities of wealth and power. These researchers recognize that most public discussions about gender are in fact debates about power—controversies over what society expects of women and men, and clashes over contrasting beliefs about social privilege and control. Their analysis, therefore, focuses less on the *content* of gender differences than on this relationship between gender and social dominance.

This approach emphasizes that cultures create the social category of gender by setting out different roles and obligations for women and for men. Anthropologists, for example, remind us that the *content* of gender roles—the precise behaviors and activities assigned to men and women—can differ widely from group to group. But the *social status* of gender roles shows little variation across cultures: roles seen as feminine—no matter their content—are ranked of lower status than those assigned to men. To take a contemporary example: in the United States the occupation of physician, which until quite recently was open almost exclusively to men, enjoys high social status. In Russia and China, where most doctors are women, the social rank of the physician is much lower. The significant difference here is not the profession, or even the level of training, but the gender of the practitioner.

Following this approach, researchers suggest that even the *psychological* differences discovered between women and men reflect the *social reality* of boys and girls growing up in different positions in the social hierarchy. For example, several traits seen as "feminine" can be described equally well as behavior appropriate for those in a subordinate social position—hesitancy to be assertive, willingness to defer to members of the more powerful group (men), reluctance to express anger or displeasure toward those on whom they depend for economic support (husbands, bosses, and other superiors who tend to be men).

Each of these three approaches to gender studies has strong advocates, and creative research moves forward in each perspective, adding steadily to our understanding of what sociologist Jeffery Weeks has named "the grand polarity." But as yet no clear consensus on gender similarity or difference emerges from the research. Aware that the analysis remains in flux, we will examine some suggestive evidence of how gender differences affect relationships between women and men in our culture.

Let's start by acknowledging similarities. Both men and women recognize the benefits of drawing close to others—a sense of belonging, an awareness of inclusion, the possibilities of love. Both women and men know that close relationships make demands for give-and-take, for accommodating to other people's needs, for generosity. All of us recognize the dangers that may accompany close relationships—domination, control, betrayal. But growing evidence reveals important differences between women and men in their emotional response to close relationships. These differences don't necessarily apply to *every* man or *every* women. But they emerge as *trends* or tendencies that often complicate relationships between women and men.

Different Images of Close Relationships

Each of us carries images or assumptions about how life works. These internal models help us to make sense of what happens to us and to predict the results of our behavior. In her influential study of moral development among women, Carol Gilligan has shown that women and men often carry different models for interpreting their experience. In relationships, Gilligan found, men and women often understand what is actually going on differently.

Relationships create bonds between people. Women tend to interpret these links positively, as sources of security. They see these developing connections as a supportive net holding people up and protecting them from harm. Although the situation is more complex and conflicted for a woman who has experienced emotional or physical violence from persons close to her, women characteristically approach relationships with a sense that "something good will happen here."

Men have different internal models. In the imagery of many men, bonds mean bondage. They experience close relationships as emotionally threatening. The net created by close connections feels more like a trap than a safety net. In this image, the links of relationships confine rather than sustain. Characteristically, then, many men approach close relationships with caution.

Rooted in these two different images, men and women have different concerns as they draw close to one another. For men, as Ruthellen Josselson notes in *Finding Herself,* "the fear is that others will get too close, that they will be caught and diminished. For women, wishing to be at the center of connection, the dominant fear is of being stranded, far out on the end and isolated from others."

Differences in Communication Style

Women and men often use language differently. Language serves us in several ways: We speak to make connections with other people; we speak to give and receive information. These two goals are met by different communication styles. Deborah Tannen calls the style we use when we want to make connections *rapport talk.* Rapport talk focuses on interaction between people: we fill one another in on the details of our lives; we share our inner worlds of meaning—thoughts, feelings, hopes.

The communication style we use to give and receive information Tannen calls *report talk.* Report talk focuses on factors at a greater distance from the self—factual knowledge, objective information, practical instructions. In societies where knowledge is power, report talk also negotiates status. Demonstrating how much we know and how direct is our access to information sources, report talk establishes our place in the power hierarchy of the group.

Report and rapport are essential aspects of adult experience. Being comfortable in both communication styles equips us better for both love and work. Most adults learn how to use each style, but Tannen's research shows that in the United States men and women tend to adopt a gender-specific style in *most* conversations. So women typically use a language style that cultivates closeness, and men more often use language in a way that establishes distance or protects boundaries. Both women and men become confused—and even angry—when those of the opposite gender use a different communication style.

Drawing on the work of psychologist Eleanor Maccoby, Tannen traces these preferences to childhood experiences. In childhood, boys typically play together in large groups divided according to status. In their games, boys use language to try to negotiate these status differences. High status boys will give orders, pushing other boys around to demonstrate their own prominence. Low status boys try to protect their independence by keeping others from telling them what to do. They use words to challenge the power hierarchy and to deflect put-downs sent their way.

Boys most frequently play organized games with clear rules and boundaries. Boys learn that rules are the glue that holds the game together and that vigorous verbal exchange about boundaries (Hey, that ball was out!) and rules (Your team has too many players!) is part of the game. In the culture of boyhood, language is used to question, to test, to dispute, to debate.

Girls tend to play together in smaller groups, with more face-to-face interaction and a keener sensitivity to "who belongs." In their early play experience, girls learn that talk is the glue that holds the game together. Their games tend to be more imaginative, based on stories (Let's play "Cinderella") or life situations (Let's play "going to school"). Girls' games have fewer structured rules and the rules remain flexible. Since inclusion is important, girls are often willing to change the rules (Since there are nine of us who want to play, it's ok to have five people on your side instead of four. That way nobody is left out!) or bend their interpretation (Since she's new at playing volleyball, let's give her another chance to serve. That way her feelings won't be hurt.) to keep the sense of community alive. Like boys, girls try to protect themselves when they play, but their bigger concern is that someone will be left out or that others will turn away from them.

Girls, then, learn to use language to negotiate questions of inclusion and exclusion. As women, they approach communication as a way to "get close to people." Women use rapport talk to establish empathy, deepen the sense of similarity, strengthen their bonds with other people. Many men, continuing a pattern established when they were boys, approach communication as the way to "keep people from pushing you around." Men want to avoid saying anything that can leave them vulnerable, so close rapport is not their goal in ordinary conversation. They prefer a more detached style, an objective reporting of facts and information. As adults, Tannen notes, many men come to a new relationship with a power question: Who is up and who is down here? Many women come with the question of intimacy: How close are we going to be?

Different Expectations in Friendship

Men and women bring these communication styles into their adult relationships, expecting closeness with other adults to be something like their experience of having a best friend in childhood. But girls and boys have different experiences of friendship.

As children, boys tend to play with other boys while girls play with other girls. As we noted above, little girls spend much of their play time in small groups where talking with one another is the major activity. Boys spend more time in larger groups organized around games with rules; playing the game is their major activity together. Any talking is about the game—measuring progress, encouraging participation, reinforcing or contesting the rules.

These early patterns influence adult relationships. Women friends tend to spend time together exploring their personal worlds of life and meaning. By sharing thoughts and feelings, women friends both express and strengthen their emotional connection.

Men's friendships are typically based on common experience—in the workplace, in the army, in school. Confronting a common task or enjoying common interests, men come in contact with each other. Gradually and indirectly, this association may grow into a friendship. Many men hesitate to discuss their personal life with another man, especially if the conversation might touch on areas of weakness or vulnerability. Most rely, instead, on a growing sense of loyalty and camaraderie to strengthen their connection with another man. Their connections are more about solidarity than self-disclosure.

As friends, then, men stand shoulder to shoulder more than face to face. Even literally: recall the image of men friends fishing together along a stream, or standing together at a bar, or sitting side by side at a sporting event. In contrast, recall the image of two women friends sitting across from one another, intent in conversation, or a small group of women gathered around a table talking.

So both men and women want to spend time with people they feel close to. But women expect to devote much of this time to conversation, with each party sharing personal information and life details.

Men expect that time with a friend will be spent doing things together. Conversation may well be mostly small talk or shop talk, with periods of silence to be expected.

In relationships between women and men, these differences cause confusion. Many women, as Lillian Rubin's research reveals, report that a man friend is not as forthcoming in sharing information about himself as they would like. Many men, on the other hand, indicate that they sometimes feel pressured by a woman friend to reveal more of themselves than is comfortable for them.

Candid discussion of these differences is not easy because, as Tannen has shown, men and women evaluate relationships differently. Most women judge that a relationship is strong when you can talk about it: when the parties can speak directly to one another about what is going on between them. But for most men, a sign that a relationship is strong is you don't have to talk about it!

Dealing with Sexual Attraction in Relationships

Many heterosexual women report close and satisfying relationships with gay and lesbian friends. Fewer heterosexual men report lesbians or gay men among the people they are close to. Gay men and lesbians, like straight people, differ widely in their patterns of friendship. Some have friends only among other gay people, but many—especially lesbians—report warm friendships with both women and men, gay and straight. So, in U.S. culture at least, women seem easier with the demands of friendship and perhaps more adept at meeting these. But men and women agree that sexual attraction often complicates cross-gender heterosexual friendships.

As we've seen in earlier chapters, *eros* includes the full range of attraction and responsiveness that draws people together. These delightful dynamics span the incredible range of arousals we experience as embodied persons. Eros encompasses the soothing sensuality of a hot bath as well as the emotional companionship of a close friend; both the delight of a good meal and the genital pleasure of lovemaking express eros. But as women and men, we often interpret the erotic possibilities of friendship in quite different ways.

In many men's experience, eros is linked with genital response. When the excitement of meeting an attractive woman includes physical arousal, a man often interprets the "chemistry" between them as essentially sexual. So his response is likely to have strong sexual overtones. Only as the friendship progresses will he feel safe enough to explore the possibility of emotional intimacy—a deeper sharing of self through significant self-disclosure.

For most women, a friendship begins first at an emotional level. They look forward to establishing connections of empathy, care, and companionship. Even when a woman is physically attracted to a man, her emotional attraction to him is what tells her friendship is possible here. As the friendship deepens, she may want to include sexual intimacy as part of the relationship. But for most women, emotional closeness comes before and opens the way for genital sharing. Many men experience these two aspects of eros in reverse order: for them, sexual attraction comes before and opens the way to a deeper emotional connection.

This difference complicates friendships. Feeling drawn to a woman, a man may "sexualize" the relationship in a way that surprises the woman (sex is not what she thought was drawing them together) or seems inappropriate to her. Her disinterest or reluctance to move the relationship toward genital expression may lead him to question whether she is as involved in the relationship as he is. In many cases the friendship moves beyond this potential standoff only when the partners are able to look at and resolve the question of how emotional closeness and erotic (even if not genital) expression come together for them.

In her research, Letty Pogrebin found that as friendships between women and men deepened, these sexual tensions diminished. Men and women here reported a shared realization: that having "sex would ruin their relationship" and that "their friendship is more precious than libido."

Men and Women as Partners

Partnership is an experience of shared power—the genuine interplay of strengths and limitations in the movement toward common goals. Partnership does not demand strict mathematical equality, but it does require real mutuality: the giving and receiving go both ways. In partnerships, each of us brings something of worth to the relationship; each receives something of value as well. Partners recognize and respect this mutual exchange of gifts.

American cultural ideals of self-sufficiency make this kind of interdependence suspect. To many of us, *interdependence* suggests that we are not strong enough to stand alone, that we *need* other people. To look to other people for emotional support or practical assistance contradicts our prevailing norms of adult maturity. U.S. culture's commitment to the frontier virtues of "making it on our own" and "being beholden to no one" can be seen most sharply in the tendency to consider *dependence* a feminine trait. Counting on other people for support and assistance is "womanly"—hardly a preferred attribute of the red-blooded American male.

But working together effectively demands that we depend on one another. This kind of *dependability* relies on a sense of personal power, not weakness. To be dependable, we must be aware of our own ability. We must trust that our resources will be there when we need them, when other people need them. This confidence is rooted in an appreciation of our own strengths—the conviction that our resources are adequate to the tasks we face.

Mature *depend-ability* also means we can rely on other people. We cannot always "go it alone." And, even more significantly, we don't have to. Here is the core of interdependence: we can count on the resources of other people as well as our own. We do not possess alone all that brings meaning and joy and accomplishment to life. We need strengths beyond our own. To ask for, to accept these resources does not demean us. Instead this interdependence opens us to the rich possibilities of partnership.

Many factors help defeat this kind of partnership between men and women. Here again, U.S. culture gives women and men different messages. The man who does not seem to need other people (especially as portrayed in the cultural icons of the cowboy, the private detective, the wealthy and successful "self-made man") is powerfully attractive. Such a man, we learn, is to be admired, courted, and accepted. Under the influence of these cultural stereotypes, men connect their masculinity with an independent stance that says, "When I appear strong and independent, others will find me desirable." This independence shields him from the demands of partnership.

In our culture's expectations, a woman may hear a different message. To appear autonomous, to act independently, is to jeopardize her femininity. She learns that dependency is attractive, that "needing to be taken care of" makes her desirable. In many situations, "being taken care of" is the easiest way or even the *only* way she can establish connections with a man. Many women, then, learn that being dependent on men is rewarding. "Coming on strong" will only put her at a disadvantage.

These constraints work against partnership in a work setting. Under the sway of cultural images of masculinity, a man may feel that he must preserve an image of self-sufficiency on the job. He may be able to develop an effective working relationship with a woman whose position is clearly subordinate—his secretary, even a junior colleague. The obvious power difference here will protect him from the risks of professional parity or the even more threatening demands of emotional mutuality. In such a world, a man will experience a woman colleague who moves toward greater partnership as a challenge.

A woman, too, may feel some strain in the move toward partnership at work. She is likely to be well acquainted with both the limits and the benefits of the subordinate role. The scope of her contribution may be narrow, but so is her responsibility if things go wrong. Unable to pursue her own vision or test the full range of her abilities, she is nonetheless shielded from the embarrassment of public failure. As learner, as apprentice, as protégée, she participates in the interplay of power from a protected position. But as a work partner, she participates more directly in the contact sport of effective collaboration—and she has both its victories and its injuries on her record.

Partnership can be threatening in the more personal relationships of friendship or marriage, as well. As long as his wife is dependent on him financially, a man may feel safe in the emotional web of attachment and belonging that holds them together. If her economic dependence is less clear (should she decide to go back to work or pursue advancement in her career), the emotional bonds between them may seem jeopardized. This shift in her obvious financial dependence has disturbed the balance of power.

Both women and men feel the stress of this shift toward partnership. When his wife goes back to work, a man may complain that she doesn't need him anymore. At the same time his wife senses that she needs him even more now—for emotional support to build her confidence, for practical assistance around the house, for collaboration in parenting. Or a woman, clearly competent to take care of herself and her job, will lament, "I don't want to do this without him." She wants to stay connected with her partner; she wants their relationship to endure and even deepen in this new context of interdependence.

For many men, the challenge of partnership is to allow themselves to acknowledge greater dependence—to be willing to admit that they need others. For many women, the challenge is to develop greater strengths of mature independence—the ability to trust their own power. For both women and men, partnership demands fresh forms of living and working together.

REFLECTIVE EXERCISE

First, respond to these questions, from the perspective of your own experience of gender. Then you may find it useful to compare your responses with others, both men and women.

For me, the main benefits of being a woman (or a man) are:

In my experience, the chief burdens that come with being a man (or a woman) are:

Over the past few years, a significant change in my understanding of myself as a woman (or a man) is:

One of the ways that being a man (or a woman) influences my spiritual life is:

ADDITIONAL RESOURCES

The extent and significance of differences between men and women generate considerable discussion. The work of Carol Gilligan and her colleagues remains central in this debate; see her *In a Different Voice* and the volume by Jill Taylor, Carol Gilligan, and Amy Sullivan, *Between Voice and Silence: Women and Girls, Race and Relationship.* For an alternative view of the relationship between gender and "voice," see Susan Harter, *The Construction of the Self: A Developmental Perspective.*

John Nicholson reviews the research record in *Men and Women: How Different Are They?* David C. Geary rejects the theory of culturally determined gender roles in favor of explanations rooted in evolutionary biology; see his *Male and Female: The Evolution of Human Sex Differences.* In *Men and Women in Interaction: Reconsidering the Differences,* Elizabeth Aries examines a wide variety of factors that influence gender differences. Peter Filene explores the shifts in gender identity that characterize contemporary American society in *Him/Her/Self.*

In *The Two Sexes: Growing Apart, Coming Together,* Eleanor E. Maccoby shows how slight differences between girls and boys develop into deep-seated adolescent convictions about gender, convictions that are brought under question by adult experience. Deborah Tannen demonstrates how these differences affect communication styles in *You Just Don't Understand: Women and Men in Conversation;* see also her *I Only Say This Because I Love You: How the Way We Talk Can Make or Break Relationships.*

Ellyn Kaschak explores the impact of gender on women's development in *Engendered Lives: A New Psychology of Women's Experience.* Jean Baker Miller's *Toward a New Psychology of Women* continues to shape the significant research agenda of the Stone Center at Wellesley College; see the Stone Center *Works in Progress* newsletter for research updates on relationship issues affecting both women and men.

In *I Know Just What You Mean,* Ellen Goodman and Patricia O'Brien explore what makes women's friendships special; they include a chapter on differences between men's and women's friendships. Lillian Rubin examines psychological dynamics between women and men in *Just Friends.* For fuller treatments of women's friendships, see Letty Cottin Pogrebin, *Among Friends,* and Sandy Sheehy, *Connecting: The Enduring Power of Women's Friendship.* Peter Nardi brings together a collection of research essays in *Men's Friendships: Research on Men and Masculinities.* We take up some of the issues of partnership between women and men in our book *The Promise of Partnership: A Model for Collaborative Ministry.*

10

Faces of the Feminine

BECOMING A WOMAN MEANS recognizing oneself in the picture of femininity that our culture paints. We may enthusiastically embrace this image of woman or reject its demands as limiting or demeaning or—more likely—do some of each. This is the process of gender identification, coming gradually to a confident sense of what it means *for me* to be a woman.

As we saw in Chapter 3, gender moves us beyond biology toward social norms and cultural ideals. If sex encompasses female and male (the biological systems that are part of the reproductive process), gender includes *masculinity* and *femininity* (understandings of what is appropriate for men and for women).

Femininity, then, is a social script—a widely shared set of expectations about the public roles and personal behaviors that are appropriate for women. The description of femininity may differ from culture to culture, but her own society's script announces to every woman in advance what she should expect of being a woman.

Western culture's script has been shaped by a mythic triad: virgin, mother, crone. These faces of the feminine appear throughout Indo-European history to our own day—in Greek and Roman mythology, in folktales and in high art, in the libretto of classic opera and in the script of television's popular "soaps." This pervasive image of femininity influences a woman's sense of herself—who she is, what she is about, what hopes and obligations are hers by right.

The traditional sketch of this feminine triptych has been drawn from a man's perspective. Since it is a man's experience of a woman's life that is represented, what we learn from the classic representations is less about women's lives than about how women are seen by men. So the *virgin* depicts the innocent young girl: beautiful for men to behold, preserving herself sexually inviolate as she awaits her destiny as wife. The *mother* appears as the strong adult women, devoted to the needs of her husband and sons. The *crone* reveals the ambiguous figure of the older woman: now bereft of beauty, beyond her productive years as wife and mother, burdensome to those around her . . . and yet mysteriously powerful, even somehow dangerous.

This symbolic representation of woman comes under serious criticism today. Tracing many contemporary distortions in man–woman relationships back to this classic schema, some critics urge that the underlying image of virgin-mother-crone be jettisoned altogether. But psychologists remind us that myths function at a level of consciousness not readily responsive to political condemnation. Symbols endure because they speak to us at a deep level; images retain their power over time because they resonate with our own life experience. The mythic structure of virgin-mother-crone, even when obscured by its heavy overlay of limiting expectations, still discloses something core to the life experience of many women. Encouraged by this awareness, women are retelling this classic Western myth, now in feminine voice.

This retelling begins with an alteration in language, changing the terminology used to identify the dimensions of women's experience. Instead of virgin, a word heavy with sexual connotation, the new story describes a woman's early sense of herself as *maiden. Mother* remains an image central in the retelling, even as the scope of the metaphor expands to include women's wider experience of their adult power. And for the third feminine face, *wise woman* replaces the disparaging term *crone.*

This narrative speaks to women at two levels, chronological and psychological. On the one hand, the symbol of maiden-mother-wise woman charts a chronological journey from young adulthood through mature age. More profoundly, these images embody enduring elements of a woman's identity: resources of self-awareness and strengths of soul that are potentially available to a woman throughout her life, even if particular circumstances of crisis or support are crucial in bringing these strengths into play. So a twenty-five-year-old woman may emerge precociously wise from an early personal trauma, while a woman in her fifties may find that not until her grown children leave home does she have the psychological and practical freedom to explore, in the maiden's stance, the possibilities of her own life's dream.

Maiden

Maiden, as both a chronological and psychological reality, describes a woman's experience of finding out who she is, who she might (still) become. The maiden is free and innocent: free in that her life remains open to possibilities, not yet determined by the compelling commitments of love and work that both strengthen and circumscribe adult identity. Her innocence is rooted less in sexual naiveté than in a sense of wonder; her experience is fresh so she sees the world as new, savors her own life as pregnant with promise.

The maiden's quest often takes an inner focus. Exploring her own potential, she asks, "How am I special?" In this pursuit she confronts the paradox of power: mature strength has roots in receptivity. U.S. culture glorifies the vigorous action and determined control that characterize adult endeavor, to the neglect of the complementary truth: life often has a schedule that cannot be rushed. Whether discerning a life's dream or following the artist's muse or carrying a baby to term, creativity takes its own time. The maiden's quest inducts her into the asceticism of patience—"waiting to give birth."

But waiting is not all. As a gift of her experience as maiden—whether a chronological time or a psychological season—a woman learns to say the *selective yes*. The maiden's task is to discover her uniqueness; she completes the quest by affirming her identity in the crucible of choice. In folktales, for example, the princess selects her mate from among all the princes of the land as she assumes her rightful place as queen. From all the possibilities she has glimpsed in the time of fertile exploration, she must now construct an actual life.

To be who she is most authentically, a women has to choose. Many women report a profound awareness, in the midst of making such a critical life decision, that their *yes* comes as a response. They experience themselves as chosen and cherished—by the beloved, by destiny, by God. In response, a woman readies herself for defining commitments that—like all genuine choice—will both affirm and limit her life. Her courage to say the selective yes is rooted in this sense of call.

Many young women today feel overwhelmed by the choices they face, with little sense of inner call or outer support to help establish priorities. So many possibilities are open to a woman, so many apparently conflicting designs of how she might live her life. Clear gender roles—carrying expectations that many in her grandmother's generation embraced and many in her mother's generation rejected—have disintegrated. In their place she finds multiple options, making mutually contradictory demands, with few clues to guide her toward trustworthy decisions. Without support to explore her experience, without reflective space in which to identify her own dream, the possibilities just leave her confused. She longs for the patience and courage that come as the maiden's gifts.

Many older women report missing the season of the maiden in their own lives. The oldest girl in a large family, for example, moved quickly into the role of "little mother" helping to raise her younger brothers and sisters. Another woman, growing up a dutiful daughter, sensed that her future was circumscribed by her parents' expectations, leaving little room for exploring her own dreams. Other women, marrying young or devoting themselves early to a service vocation or other demanding career, find themselves inducted quickly into the compelling tasks of meeting other people's needs. For these and many other women, not until midlife do they meet the maiden within.

The maiden arrives along various paths. As young adult children leave home, their mother returns to college, eager to immerse herself in the world of books and ideas. A woman, surviving a troubled childhood by turning away from her memories of physical or emotional abuse, begins therapy as a step in a long-resisted journey of healing. During a sabbatical semester away from her customary ministry, a woman religious experiences the resurgence of an earlier dream to live in greater solidarity with the poor; with some trepidation, she determines to follow this dream to see where it will lead her. A successful executive, recuperating from major surgery, resolves to simplify her lifestyle so that she has time to consider her hopes for the rest of her life. Each of these scenarios reflects a woman's sense of possibility, her openness to change, her courage on the inner quest. No matter her chronological age, each woman here welcomes the maiden's summons.

Mother

Moving beyond maiden, the image of mother celebrates the strong adult woman intensely involved in life-giving tasks of creativity and care. At this stage a woman no longer sees herself as free and innocent; she recognizes instead that she is *committed* and *knowledgeable.* Whatever the shape of her lifestyle, a woman composes her life through commitments made and remade. She initiates plans, attempts relationships, survives both failure and success. People daily depend on her for nurturance and support. Deserving voices—family and friends, clients and co-workers, projects in crisis and people in need—all announce insistent claims. These multiple obligations test her talent and resolve, even as they strengthen her connections with people and enhance her sense of contributing to the world. But innocence does not serve these adult commitments well. As mother, a woman seeks to know more so that she may care well for all that is in her charge.

As mother, too, she learns to say the *generous yes.* Her asceticism here differs from the maiden's. The maiden must choose selectively among multiple options, lest the allure of "all that is possible" distract her from the task of taking up life in the real world of limits. As mother, she must learn to respond generously to multiple needs, lest the fragile possibilities of the new life in her care be lost.

Parenting is an open-ended commitment. Mothers seldom sense themselves choosing selectively which of their baby's needs to meet or determining in advance the limits beyond which their active concern will not go. Nurturing new life requires a more generous response. As mother, a woman tries to ready herself for *whatever* is needed, whatever the growth and safety and well-being of her children will require of her. As spouse or friend, too, a woman opens herself to demands that can't be fully calculated ahead of time.

Women learn the disciplines of nurturance in the work world as well. As leaders or colleagues, as workers or managers, as artists or teachers or healers, women initiate and foster life. Like parenting, tending "the works of my hands" teaches women—and men—the paradox of creativity. Generating life demands ongoing discernment, as we learn to *hold on* as long as helpful and to *let go* as soon as needed. Only in this delicate balance does our strength serve new life on its own terms.

Finding in herself the resources for such sensitivity and generosity is a glory for most women. But working with women in support groups and therapy sessions and spiritual direction has made many counselors cautious of the encompassing claims of the mother symbol. Nurturance is not the only strength a women finds in herself; being mother is not her full identity. When *mother* becomes the dominant script of femininity, "other people's needs" risk becoming the defining focus in a woman's life. To be feminine, then, is to meet— even to anticipate—these needs.

Making *care for others* the chief characteristic of femininity can be dangerous both to women and to those in their care. Women who accept that self-definition quickly find themselves overwhelmed by frustration and guilt. Other people's needs are endless; no guidelines exist for when we've done enough. If taking care of others defines what being a woman means, taking care of herself becomes suspect. In this milieu, a women who gives energy to her own development and well-being is seen as selfish, often even by herself. When the needs of others claim clear moral precedence, a woman takes time off only reluctantly. Even then, leisure seems acceptable only as a way of recharging her energy for a return to the caregiver role.

But maturity introduces a woman into a complex realm of moral discernment and compromise, as she weighs multiple commitments. For many women it is in the struggle to mediate among these many valid claims, balancing her own hopes and the demanding needs of others, that she touches new resources in herself. The wise woman begins to emerge.

Wise Woman

The wise woman has learned the source of her significance. Beyond her important contributions to others—giving birth, nurturing life, caring for the needs of the world—she is valuable for herself. This spiritual transformation is often triggered by a dramatic shift in a woman's life circumstances—the death of her parents or spouse, her own children leaving home and establishing separate—even distant— lives, an estrangement from people close to her as she pursues new personal goals, or the shock of serious illness. In these events, aloneness confronts a woman in new ways. Separation threatens the network of close connections that previously sustained her, challenging who she is and what she stands for. But gazing into this dark mirror of solitude, the wise woman recognizes a faithful ally—herself.

Affirming that she is strong enough to stand apart liberates a woman. For most women this demanding freedom is only slowly won. Long relied on by other people, a woman gradually comes to count herself reliable. Her intuition, proved trustworthy over time, becomes a credible resource. Now she knows her insights can be trusted. In her own life, experience has ripened into wisdom.

Supported by this strength, a woman approaches decisions differently. Now when complex issues of meaning or value or choice arise, she draws on a new authoritative perspective—the seasoned insight born of her own experience. Other sources of information are not simply ignored, but she weighs their claims more carefully. Confident in her personal convictions, she is not easily dismissed. The wise woman demands to be taken seriously.

In this season—chronological or psychological—a woman becomes more self-directed. Her attention is less focused outside herself—on meeting social expectations, on pleasing the people around her, on anticipating their needs. To those who have become accustomed to benefiting from her devoted concern, she may even appear "indifferent." She is at least unacceptably indifferent to them, since she does not so regularly drop everything else and come when she is called!

In this season, too, many women regain their assertiveness. Most women learn early the disciplines of accommodation, setting aside personal needs for the sake of others and moderating anger so relationships are not harmed. The wise woman holds her relationships and her responsibilities in new ways. Balancing selectively these various demands, she determines how to give herself to others and when to direct her energies elsewhere. She is more open to confrontation, less intimidated by her own or other people's anger. And no longer reluctant to speak her own truth, she willingly risks being branded as unladylike: opinionated, overbearing, pushy.

Practiced in the maiden's *yes* of selective choice and mother's *yes* of generous response, it is in this season that a woman learns to say *no*. Her noncompliance is not the petulance of the child nor an adolescent's rebellion but the moral *no* that defends life's larger truths. She says no to external expectations: society's demands that women conform to a singular image of femininity—passive, unobtrusive, helpful, self-effacing, demure. She says no to the needs of others: sometimes for their benefit, so that those in her care find their own resources and outgrow their dependence on her; sometimes for her benefit, as she respects her own needs and leaves behind the wearying effort to prove herself indispensable, to ground her worth in other people's approval.

Discerning the moral *no* equips the wise woman for the tasks of responsible renunciation. She approaches aging and death having learned to embrace the inevitable purifications of change, to grieve what must be let go, and to welcome the gift that often awaits on the other side of loss.

Hers is often the prophetic *no*. As a woman, she knows the burdens society imposes on those it casts as socially inferior. Seeing through this sham of discrimination and injustice, she dares to challenge the pretenses of power. Her resistance is fueled by a deeper source of freedom. No longer hostage to other people's expectations, ready to stand alone and apart if need be, the wise woman has nothing to lose. No wonder conventional society casts the crone as an threatening figure: she is dangerous to the status quo!

Many of us recall the childhood story "The Emperor's New Clothes." The gullible ruler relies on greedy counselors who siphon off the kingdom's riches for their own use. As the day of the emperor's coronation approaches, the treasury has no funds to purchase a fitting cloak for the ruler to wear. The guileful counselors convince the young ruler that they have, in fact, obtained a splendid cloak for him to wear, made of thread so fine that only the truly regal can even see it. Reluctant to admit that he cannot see the cloak and risk exposing his royal inadequacy, the ruler sets out naked along the parade route to the coronation site. The common people who line the way are shocked and dismayed to see their ruler naked. But, fearing the wrath of the treacherous advisors who parade with the ruler and proclaim the beauty of his imperial cloak, the crowd goes along with the deceit. In the usual telling of the story, an innocent child breaks their evil hold on the crowd by calling out the obvious truth, "the emperor has no clothes." But in other versions of the story, a wizened older woman of the village plays this prophetic role. It is not a child's innocence but the crone's courage that breaks the hold of social pretense.

Confirmed in the truth of her own experience, supported by the sisterhood of other wise women, she is "fierce with the reality of age," a formidable force for institutional purification and social change.

The classic Western myth of femininity is being transformed as women give witness to their own experience. Christianity's long-cherished image of woman, celebrated in Mary as virgin/mother, is likewise being expanded by women of faith. As maidens exploring new identities for themselves in church and society, as mothers responding creatively to the world's cry of need, as wise women acting courageously in renewal and reform, faithful women today enlarge the church's understanding of itself and its mission. If she would welcome all these faces of the feminine, Mother Church could herself stand as model of Wise Woman for the world.

REFLECTIVE EXERCISE

Recall some of the heroines who shaped your imagination as you were growing up. Perhaps a figure from a fairy tale: Cinderella or Snow White or Sleeping Beauty. Or a character in a novel: Alice in Wonderland or Heidi or Nancy Drew. Your heroine may have been a religious saint or a public celebrity or someone in your own family.

Choose one of these early heroine figures who was significant for you. First, make a list of the qualities that you, when you were young, found most interesting or most admirable about her. Give some examples of these qualities "in action."

Then reflect on your heroine figure again, now from the perspective of your life these days. What about your early heroine is attractive or interesting to you now? Have you taken on any of her qualities in your own life? Has your evaluation of her changed in any way?

ADDITIONAL RESOURCES

In *Woman: An Intimate Geography,* Natalie Angier provides a readable summary of current research findings on biological, emotional, and social aspects of women's experience. Carol Tavris corrects some of the misinformation and myths of femininity in *The Mismeasure of Women. Sexuality, Society, and Feminism,* edited by Cheryl Brown Tarvis and Jacquelyn W. White, offers a state-of-the-art review of psychological research examining the interplay among women's experience and social and cultural settings. In *Women and Human Development: The Capabilities Approach,* philosopher Martha Nussbaum proposes an ethical basis for international development, taking seriously the concrete reality of women's lives.

Beyond Appearances: A New Look at Adolescent Girls, edited by Norine Johnson, Michael Roberts, and Judith Worell, gives a balanced look at both the strengths of teenage girls and the challenges they face in the move into adult life. Psychologist Ruthellen Josselson traces the developmental journey from adolescence into midlife in *Finding Herself: Pathways to Identity Development in Women* and *Revising Herself: The Story of Women's Identity from College to Midlife*. Lillian Rubin examines the movement beyond midlife in *Tangled Lives: Daughters, Mothers and the Crucible of Aging;* see also *Lesbians at Midlife: The Creative Transition* by Barbara Sang, Joyce Warshov, and Adrienne Smith, and *Suddenly Sixty* by Judith Viorst. Sondra Forsyth and Carol Gilligan draw on the wisdom of mature women role models in *Girls Seen and Heard: Life Lessons for Our Daughters*.

Maria Harris serves as a trustworthy guide for women on the spiritual journey; see her *Dance of the Spirit: The Seven Steps of Women's Spirituality* and *Jubilee Time: Celebrating Women, Spirit and the Advent of Age*. Kathleen Fischer's work describes and supports an empowering spirituality for women; see *Women at the Well: Feminist Perspectives on Spiritual Direction, Autumn Gospel: Women in the Second Half of Life,* and *Transforming Fire: Women Using Anger Creatively*. In *Women's Spirituality: Resources for Christian Development,* Joann Wolski Conn offers a splendid collection of essays highlighting women's spiritual resources. Catherine Mowry LaCugna brings together a series of essays illuminating major theological issues in *Freeing Theology: The Essentials of Theology in Feminist Perspective*. Lisa Sowle Cahill explores connections between women's sexual and spiritual experience in *Women and Sexuality*.

11

Scripts for Masculinity

B ORN MALE, MEN ARE RECRUITED into the ways of masculinity. Having inherited the genes that define our biological sex, we gradually learn the roles and rules assigned to our gender. Through its treasure trove of fables and customs, of celebrated rogues and well-remembered heroes, our society introduces us to models of manhood—some as ideal scripts, others as cautionary tales. With this cultural guidance, our identities as men are socialized and shaped.

These scripts include expectations and guidelines for "acting like a man." In *Body and Society,* his masterful study of sexuality in the first centuries of the Christian church, historian Peter Brown gives examples of one culture's masculinity script. For the citizens of second-century Rome, Brown notes, "it was never enough to be male: a man had to aspire to remain virile." Many aspects of men's lives have changed between second-century Rome and twenty-first-century United States: togas have given way to trousers and sport utility vehicles replace chariots. But some criteria of virility remain the same.

> The small town notables of the second century watched each other with hard, clear eyes. They noted a man's walk. They reacted to the rhythms of his speech. They listened attentively to the telltale resonance of his voice.

Both in the Roman Empire and in contemporary America, achieving manhood is fraught with peril. Recognizing how important it is to fit in, we must quickly learn the rules of membership. So we watch and imitate our models, striving to be accepted as men. Like the Romans before us, it may well be in the measure of our walk and the pitch of our voice that our manhood will be judged.

An unsettling question plagues the pursuit of masculinity: "Am I man enough?" A man's career as a nurse or primary school teacher might prod this doubt. A religious calling that includes the lifestyle of celibacy could raise this question. A gay man reads the signals in a heterosexual culture and wonders, "Am I man enough?" Because the criteria of manliness are so exacting (and constantly marketed in the era of Viagra), no man is safe. Does being bald compromise my virility? If I am childless, have I failed a test of manliness? How much money do I need to make to be a *real man*?

The example of mature men who have followed alternative scripts for manhood enriches a culture's conversation about masculinity: a man with clear artistic or academic talent but little interest in sports or automobiles; a gay man who refuses to closet himself in heterosexual society and lives instead with open integrity; a married man who delights in his wife's professional success and shares the responsibilities of family and household. Christians have the extraordinary witness of Jesus, who, unmarried and without children, forged a life whose paradoxical fruitfulness did not conform to the conventional standards of his own time—or ours.

The autobiographical story *A River Runs Through It* presents a poignant portrait of a masculinity script. The author's father is a Protestant minister with a passion for fly fishing. The story begins: "In our family there was no clear line between religion and fly fishing." In the stream near their house, the father instructs his two sons in the intricacies of this art: where to stand, how to flick the wrist precisely, so that the lure lands just where you want. The young sons watch and imitate their father. Standing in the stream side by side—as men are wont—they learn to act like their father. Then, as good competitors, they strive to out-perform him. In this simple ritual, they rehearse a script for manhood.

Scripts have a great advantage: they show us how to act. Following paths that have been successful before, we are not simply left on our own. Ronald Levant, for example, reports on the work of the Society for the Psychological Study of Men and Masculinity, helping men recognize the resources of self-reliance, loyalty, problem-solving skills, and assertiveness that are part of a vital masculine script.

But cultural scripts are likely to harden over time into codes—strictly regulated patterns of acting, without much room for improvisation or flexibility. A code is meant to elicit an automatic response. Think of the significance of "code blue" in a hospital setting. This alarm is not an invitation to discuss the patient's health; rather it signals an emergency that requires immediate predetermined action.

A code attracts us to its simplicity and clarity. The value lies in its guaranteed response, especially useful in medical or military emergencies. But when a vital conversation ("What does it mean to be a man?"), once expressed in lively scripts ("Here are credible ways to be a worker, or become a father, or behave as a citizen"), becomes compressed into an automatic response ("Act this way, or else . . ."), the code finally stymies us. Our actions may meet the requirements of a "real man," but our behavior feels empty and repetitive. Even as we conform, we sense the stagnation.

Sex is often the focus when men report their own experience of masculinity scripts that have degenerated into codes. They speak of three cultural expectations that are particularly damaging to men's sense of themselves and to their relationships. The first is the imperative that men must be the initiators in any sexual exchange. This is their role. Any variation of this code of behavior only threatens their adequacy. One of the blessings of marriage is that a man can learn that genuine mutuality means both partners can initiate and respond; in this sacred space, rigid gender rules can be set aside.

A second sexual script encourages men—adolescents and adults—to see casual sex as their prerogative. Adolescent males are "expected" to experiment sexually, often without much emotional involvement or concern for consequences. The dangerous lesson embedded in such behavior is that sex and love have separate lives. A young woman who is similarly sexually active suffers more negative consequences, both in the burden of unwanted pregnancy (since the masculine code lays upon her all responsibility for birth control) and in social disdain (consider the vocabulary of abuse and condemnation still used against a woman who "sleeps around"). This double standard becomes painfully obvious in the realm of pornography. In most cultures it is acceptable (even if publically denounced) that men would enjoy this disengaged style of sexual arousal. That a man's sister or girlfriend or daughter would appear in a pornographic display is, however, intolerable—an insult to *his* masculinity.

Perhaps the most damaging aspect of the masculine sexual code is the fusion of sexuality and genital expression. Many men learn that sexuality *means* genital expression. A friendly smile in the office is seen as a sexual come-on; a supportive hug from a friend must signal an invitation to have sex. The range of human sensuality and affection—from the various delights of sight and touch and taste to the simple pleasures of friendship—is reduced to genital activity. Following this script over time, many men come to a painful realization: this frenetic focus on genital expression has impoverished their relationships and diminished their wider enjoyment of life.

Masculine Detachment

In his book *Real Boys,* William Pollack traces ways the cultural scripts for manhood in America easily slip into burdensome codes of behavior, which he calls "masks of masculinity." His research focuses on the myths of boyhood in which the code of masculinity originates. For Pollack, the healthy cultural imperatives that urge a boy to "stand on his own two feet" often end by disconnecting the boy from his emotional life. The script for independence degenerates into a code of emotional detachment.

To understand the roots of this process, Pollack turns to Nancy Chodorow's analysis of child-rearing dynamics, which we examined in Chapter 4. An early lesson for the human infant, common to both girls and boys, comes as an initial blow to narcissism: my mother is not me! This person who cares for me is not just an extension of myself. She has a separate existence that often shifts her attention away from satisfying my needs. Wounded by this necessary injury to his infantile sense of omnipotence, the boy-child soon recognizes a second confusing truth: not only is he *not* his mother; as male, he is *not like* his mother. If the girl-child can take comfort in being nurtured by someone with whom she can identify as a woman, the boy-child's journey to manhood leads him to separate himself more extensively from his mother.

Pollack's research suggests that the American script for manhood reinforces this premature separation. From his early years, parents often instruct their son "to be a big boy," not to cry, not to cling to his parents, not to be so needy. This early and enforced detachment leads many young men to a disconnect from their emotions.

Composure

Psychologist Adam Phillips explores the masculine code of emotional detachment under the intriguing rubric of *composure*. Usually we don't notice the phenomenon of composure until some sudden social embarrassment strips it away. For example, we make a verbal slip in the midst of an important meeting—losing our train of thought or mispronouncing someone's name. Suddenly we are confused and flustered; perhaps we blush or stutter or break into a sweat. We lose our composure. Unsettled by this loss of equanimity and control, we struggle to gather our wits and "get our act together." After a moment or two, we have regained our composure.

These painful but transitory experiences remind us how essential composure is. Without what Phillips calls a "calculated social poise," confidence eludes us. So composure plays a significant role in the script for adult maturity. But for some men this necessary strength becomes a liability. No longer a healthy way of *self-holding*, their composure instead secures a more detached style of *self-hiding*. Some men develop a relationship style that keeps other people at a well-defended distance. This calculated aloofness communicates "a relative absence of neediness." In Phillips's clinical experience, such apparent self-possession is often guided by "a fantasy of self-sufficiency, in which desire for the other is interpreted as concession to the other." Here composure ends by isolating a man from the very persons he wishes to be near.

Acknowledging that self-defeating composure remains part of the code of masculinity, Phillips still concludes his reflections on an optimistic note. Perhaps, he suggests, men hold to this style of severe detachment, awaiting an environment in which their composure will no longer be necessary. Hiding behind our aloofness and apparent self-sufficiency, we long for the safe setting where we can surrender our composure and find the intimacy we hunger for.

Masculinity's code of detachment does not stop with distant relationships. Men often find they have become disconnected from their own feelings. The Fatherhood Project at Boston University studied young fathers in a variety of exchanges with their own children. These interactions were videotaped and later reviewed by the men themselves. The fathers frequently responded that not until they *saw themselves on tape* were they aware of the many feelings these interchanges with their children had aroused in them.

As men become detached from their feelings, they are inclined to fall silent. Wives frequently complain that their husbands do not share what they are feeling. Pollack observed that as the young boys in his research became teenagers, they characteristically would "lose their voice." Carefree and spontaneous expression of feelings drains from their lives. But this is not a problem reserved for adolescence. Many adults have memories of silent fathers who rarely expressed any emotion. Long after a father's death, they carry questions: "What was he feeling? Did he love me?" Consider this poignant example: At a family reunion, a midlife son tells his siblings that he remembers their father reading to them. The siblings, recalling their own experiences of a taciturn and stern father, insist that this happy memory is an invention. The forty-year-old responds ruefully, "Don't you remember when he would come home from work, open up the newspaper and silently read to us?"

Why is silence so central in the code of masculinity? Many men have learned that feelings render them vulnerable. A surge of sorrow threatens to elicit tears, putting a man at a disadvantage among his male friends. Admitting he is even slightly depressed could jeopardize his job. Acknowledging disappointment over a setback could label him a failure. Silence seems a man's best defense against such vulnerability. The code of masculinity instructs him to fall silent in the face of feelings for which he has no name nor any "manly" way of expression.

But his silence speaks with great effectiveness: an angry glare during a business meeting or a resentful pause during a dinner conversation communicates a man's mood. When men cling to their silence, people close to them must decipher what men are feeling. A husband comes home from work, exhausted and silent; his wife is left to estimate his mood. Their relationship careens through shoals of his unnamed feelings until, finally, she bursts into anger or tears. So his emotional distress finds expression—vicariously. But carrying these displaced feelings quickly becomes a burden for the man's spouse and a barrier in their relationship. A participant in one of our workshops describes her experience: "I am now actively breaking away from being the provider of my husband's emotions. This is no small task! My new behavior causes friction in our relationship, but the change is forcing him to get acquainted with himself. After twenty years, I'm tired of being the interpreter of the world for him."

Competition and Control

In the script of mature adulthood, competition plays a valuable role. Competition spurs us to test our own limits, often helping us perform better than we first thought possible. In the ups and downs of competition, we learn how to win with grace and how to lose with honor. But the masculine code puts these benefits in jeopardy. For the "real man," it stipulates, winning is all. Then we start to see other people as adversaries or obstacles to our success. To get a clear picture of our competition, we need to hold people at arm's length, to size them up from a distance.

When competitiveness dominates social exchange, personal advantage becomes more important than effective collaboration. When the sole criterion of business success is the "bottom line," company loyalty fades from memory. Such a climate makes mutuality dangerous. Moving from these public settings, where emotional distance is required and an adversarial stance is reinforced, many men take their competitive strategies with them, only to find that these tactics serve them less well in the intimate realms of marriage, parenting, and friendship.

Control is a third theme of the code of masculinity. Like competition, control is crucial in adult maturing. Growing up, we must learn to control our behavior and our desires. Parents and teachers help us develop the necessary disciplines of delayed gratification. Realizing that we are more than bystanders, we try to influence what goes on around us. But control sometimes slips into coercion—a forceful, compulsive insistence that things go my way. Being "in control" like this—dominant, intimidating, manipulative—lies at the core of the masculine code.

Christian theology has long been a partner in the cultural code of control. Even the imperative in the book of Genesis to "subdue and dominate the earth" (Genesis 1:28) has seemed to legitimize men's control over all creation—including women. Early in the Christian tradition, a stoic desire to harness human emotions led to a portrait of God as passionless—too perfect to be subject to emotions that render men vulnerable. The passionate God of the Hebrew Scriptures was recast as a God of control: a serene Unmoved Mover, unaffected by the arousals of anger or regret or compassion. This novel script for God sponsored a similar spirituality for religious leaders: the Christian minister should be characterized by composure and self-control, disciplined in lifestyle, unshaken by emotional "disturbances." For the Catholic leader, the detachment went further, removing the priest from the bonds of marriage and family.

Masculine control finds special expression in the code of paternalism, still prominent in the Christian community. The leader may be friendly, eager to please, even indulgent—but nevertheless determined to do things *my way*. Paternalism is a risk endemic to leadership, surfacing in the presumption that "the leader knows best." Eager to make sure that things turn out right, the leader is tempted to make decisions for other people. And, to be sure, women in leadership positions often succumb to this risk, too.

The practice of paternalism is not limited to the leader's role. Wherever control masquerades as care, paternalism is at play. In our middle years we can feel its tug as we deal with young-adult children or assume new responsibility for our aging parents. A friend in his fifties tells this story: His elderly parents became very concerned about a financial problem that seemed minor to him. At first he listened like a good son, eager to learn the extent of the problem. But soon, frustrated by their repeated worries, he decided to take the initiative. He quickly settled the financial situation and then, pleased with the results, informed his parents. They were not pleased. Their anger alerted him to the significant flaw in his well-meaning action: he had treated his parents like children.

Christian Spirituality and Integrity

The conversation about masculinity is finally about belonging: Where do we fit in? How does a man participate effectively in the overlapping worlds of his experience—as friend and colleague? As husband and father? As contributor in church and society? The response of masculine detachment, with its code of composure and control, seems less and less satisfying. Disillusioned by this sterile ideal, men search for clues to a more vital way to live.

For many men, this search brings us first to grief. But this is not just bad news. As Robert Bly has observed—and the gospel tradition before him—the discipline of grief may serve as a door to new life. One man laments his father's death, which leaves words never spoken between them and now unspeakable. Another mourns the loss of an authoritative church whose sure control seemed to guarantee grace. A third regrets the demise of a society where women knew their proper place and men's prerogatives were uncontested. The courage to grieve these losses opens the door to transformation. Neglected values and forgotten feelings return, energizing us to explore anew our identity as men.

Identity raises the question of integrity. Integrity points to the challenge of bringing together the different aspects of our complex lives and our multifaceted selves. We need to integrate both our gifts and our wounds; we must harmonize the successes and the failures of our life. A community faces a similar challenge, to integrate its diverse members into a vital group.

Psychologist Erik Erikson suggests that integrity is the ultimate human task: in our senior years especially we are challenged to say *yes* to the unique and peculiar journey of our own lives. Both individuals and groups face this challenge of integration—to acknowledge parts of our life that have been neglected or denied, and to befriend our diversity.

In the fourth century, St. Ambrose defined the virtue of integrity in a strikingly masculine fashion. As Peter Brown recounts, the bishop of Milan pictured integrity as "the precious ability *to keep what was one's own* untarnished by alien intrusion" (our emphasis). Two elements of this vision of integrity have profoundly influenced Christian spirituality. The first is the connection between integrity and detachment. Ambrose located integrity in each person's uniqueness. Holiness lay in the individual's singularity, which must be protected from the soiling contact with others. For Ambrose, the best embodiment of this virtue was the virgin: a person who remains "intact," untouched by others. In Ambrose's vision, then, detachment became the chief vehicle of spiritual growth, meshing perfectly with the Western cultural code of masculine separateness.

The second element of Ambrose's vision was more ominous. Ambrose was concerned not only with the individual's integrity but with the church's as well. The orthodoxy and wholeness of the church were challenged in the same way that the purity of the individual was tested: the intrusion of others who tarnish one's integrity. These intrusions, which polluted the purity of the church or the individual, were described by Ambrose as *effeminizing*. In Ambrose's imagination, a dualism of church and world paralleled an opposition of masculine and feminine. In both dichotomies, integrity demanded a masculine detachment from a tarnishing contact with women.

This script for religious integrity no longer works. Detachment and control have not brought men the fruitfulness that our hearts demand. We begin to question the ideal of the virgin as prescriptive for all Christians. We ask ourselves, "What if integrity pivots not only on detachment but on the vital attachments of our lives?" Humans begin life attached. Each of us is first nurtured in a womb where we are securely tethered to our mother by a life-sustaining cord. This contact, with its intimate exchange of fluids, did not soil but sustained us. The umbilical cord is soon exchanged for the other vital attachments of our lives: to our family, to the neighborhood and other communities that shape our childhood. When we leave home we develop new inter-dependencies, forging the links of love and work and faith that con-firm us as adults. These are the engagements that define our lives and make them fruitful.

Our integrity is not preserved in isolation, untouched by the intru-sion of others. Wholeness is instead forged in connections and com-mitments. The greatest peril is not contamination by others but an isolation that leaves us intact but ungenerous, composed but alone. Our life becomes fruitful only because we are linked with others—in nurturing children, in crafting human culture, in solidarity with the poor, in stewarding the resources of the earth we share. The virtue of integrity flowers not in an inviolate privacy but in vital attachments.

Masculine spirituality today speaks of both engagement and detachment. This turn in the conversation invites us to define integrity anew: not solely as the sovereignty of one's own body but as the unity and diversity of the Body of Christ. The ancient code of mas-culinity, grounded in composure and control, breaks down. In a sea-son of shifting scripts for both women and men, we regain our confidence that (in the words of Roberto Unger) "in binding ourselves . . . to others we need not deny or dissolve our self." Empowered by this experience, we take up again the discussion of what it takes to be a man, what it means to be a woman. The conversation of Christian spirituality continues.

REFLECTIVE EXERCISE

Consider the scripts for masculinity that touch your own life. For you these days, what are the most important requirements for "acting like a man"? Has your list of requirements changed over time? Give some examples.

How does your current understanding of manhood support and strengthen you? Are there ways this script for "being a man" affects you negatively—your self-confidence or your relationships or your spirituality?

In your experience, where is pressure strongest to conform to a "code" of masculinity: at work? at church? in sexual performance? in public behavior? in friendships and family gatherings? Again, offer some examples from your own life.

ADDITIONAL RESOURCES

A River Runs Through It is Norman Maclean's moving autobiographical account of the family relationships among his father, his brother, and himself. In *Real Boys: Rescuing Our Sons from the Myths of Boyhood*, William Pollack reports findings from his own work and other research on formative influences on men's identity; see also Michael Gurian's *The Good Son: Shaping the Moral Development of Our Boys and Young Men* and *A Fine Young Man: What Parents, Mentors, Educators Can Do to Shape Adolescent Boys into Exceptional Men*.

Historian Peter Brown traces the roots of Christianity's suspicion of women and sexuality in *The Body and Society: Men, Women, and Sexual Renunciation in Early Christianity*. Brown's observation on virility appears on p. 11; he discusses Ambrose's use of "virgin" as a symbol of integrity on p. 354 and the threat of "effeminizing," on pp. 347–50. Philosopher Roberto Unger examines the significance of human emotion in *Passion: An Essay on Personality*.

In *A New Psychology of Men*, William Pollack and Ronald Levant provide a collection of papers representing the work of the Society for Psychological Study of Men and Masculinity; see also Robert Levant and Gary Brooks, *Men and Sex: New Psychological Perspectives*. Harold Kooden, in *Golden Men: The Power of Gay Midlife*, describes the challenges gay men face and the resources they develop in finding appropriate scripts for masculinity. Robert Bly explores the mythic masculine journey in *Iron John: A Book about Men*. Adam Phillips discusses composure in his book *On Kissing, Tickling, and Being Bored*.

Christie Cozad Neuger and James Newton Poling bring together a series of pastoral essays on *The Care of Men;* see especially Herbert Anderson's chapter "Men and Grief." John Carmody's discussion in *Toward a Male Spirituality* continues to illumine men's cultural experience and their spiritual quest; see also James Nelson, *The Intimate Connection: Male Sexuality, Masculine Spirituality.* Erik Erikson and Joan Erikson describe the virtue of integrity in *The Life Cycle Completed: A Review;* see also the discussion in *Vital Involvement in Old Age,* by Erik H. Erikson, Joan M. Erikson, and Helen Q. Kivnick.

12

The Place of Pleasure

*D*onnie,

    I am sending this e-mail with a lot of embarrassment. When you raised those questions about sexuality last night you caught me off-guard. I pretended to be too busy, packing for this trip, but I was really just embarrassed. Four hours on the plane this morning gave me time to think. I apologize now for how I acted yesterday.

    On the plane I was remembering that my parents never had anything to say to me about sex. (I was too shy—unlike you!—to ask.) There seemed to be an etiquette in our house: such things we never talk about! I still regret that, and I am determined things will be different with us. Please accept my stumbling efforts, in this long-distance message, to be honest with you.

    You asked especially about masturbation. Let me start with my own story. When I was fifteen, as you are now, I often felt overwhelmed by sex. I would masturbate and then hate myself for it. I was ashamed that I could not control myself. The parish priest encouraged me to pray and keep trying to overcome my "problem," but this did not seem to help much.

    I had learned that masturbation was a mortal sin, that it would separate me from God. If I died after such a sin, before confession, I would go to hell. This puzzled me and made me angry. How could something that I couldn't control damn me forever? How could it cancel out all the rest of my life? I didn't have a satisfying answer to these questions, but I was still convinced that what I was doing was a terrible sin.

In this confusing time I was surrounded mostly by silence. Both in high school and later in college my counselors were as mute as my parents. Perhaps I was the only one who sinned this way again and again! I felt isolated and defeated. In college I finally stopped confessing this "sin"—mainly because it didn't look like I would stop. It seemed stupid to keep going to confession. I suppose, too, that the behavior became less terrible to me as time went on. I suppose I blocked it out mostly, though I continued to feel ashamed that I had so little control in this part of my life.

From this ancient perch of forty-two years, what can I say about sex to my teenage son? What to say to you—who knows so much and wants to know even more? About masturbation I would say it is normal; it happens, with confusion and force, to most all adolescents—especially males. Your body is now ready for things that your mind and heart cannot handle yet. When you do experience this self-stimulation, you probably feel that it is not your finest hour. But know that it is not terrible; masturbation does not turn you into a bad person.

Maybe my best counsel is patience. Gradually sex will feel better in your life: not so out of control, not so isolating. Our worst fear, your mother's and mine, would be that this confusion about masturbation might lead you to hate your body and to mistrust it. Our best hope is that, with time and patience, you will find someone to share love and sex for a lifetime. (I don't mean SOON!)

When I get home next week I look forward to your reactions to this letter and to your other questions. Let's keep talking, Donnie, even if it is difficult.

I love you very much,
Dad

This father's letter acknowledges a painful truth: the question of masturbation confuses the young and embarrasses their parents. Christians rarely discuss it. This uneasy silence is broken only by occasional reiterations of a stern admonition—these sexual actions are always gravely sinful and shatter our relationship with God. But another wisdom grows in the body of Christ. Coming to this wisdom from the experiences of their own sexual lives, Christians nevertheless remain reluctant to enter a public debate over self-pleasuring. This is due in part to personal reticence and in part to a concern not to give this question more attention than it deserves.

Our colleagues in ministry—married and single, clergy and laity— insist that the time has come to speak frankly about this aspect of human sexuality. Many mature Christians remain burdened by guilt and shame about masturbation. A candid discussion may heal some of this distress and may also illumine other aspects of our religious maturing.

Genital self-stimulation is a common, even pervasive, human experience. The Kinsey Report in the 1940s suggested that ninety-four percent of men and more than sixty percent of woman had engaged in sexual self-stimulation. In more recent research, James McCary finds that about ninety-five percent of men and between fifty and ninety percent of women report sexual self-pleasuring. John Perito, an experienced psychiatrist and author within the Catholic tradition, judges that masturbation need not interfere with the goals of mature sexuality, but can "in fact enhance them." To these observers, genital self-pleasuring is neither aberrant nor unnatural. Such a starting point differs considerably from the attitude that flowered in the nineteenth and the first half of the twentieth century. During this period many physicians, clergy, and educators shared the conviction that masturbation was bizarre and degenerate behavior that resulted in a variety of mental and physical disorders.

A Troubled Heritage

How did Christians come to so negative a view of self-stimulation? Three currents in the church's moral thinking converged to shape its suspicion of masturbation.

The first factor was the unhappy overlap of sex and guilt. We have seen this before: all sexual behavior was judged to be "grave matter"— potentially a serious sin. The church assigned enormous importance to every arousal, each sexual fantasy. As a result, even if this was not intended, many religious people learned to be suspicious of all stirrings of sexual pleasure. We often drowned the delight of sexual arousal in a sea of shame and guilt.

A second aspect of the church's moral thinking was its focus on specific behaviors. As theologian Charles Curran has noted, our moral theology characteristically concentrated on particular behaviors—such as divorce, contraception, masturbation. In such an approach, all divorces look the same, no matter the circumstances. The separation of an immature couple does not differ from the flight of a mother and children from a violent and abusive spouse. All contraceptive acts fall under the same judgment, whatever the motivation; the discipline of the couple concerned about caring for the children they already have is not distinguishable from the self-centered decision of another couple. This moral orientation focused narrowly on behavior to the neglect of the larger context of psychological or social influences. Such concentration gives the biological act of self-pleasuring an exaggerated importance.

In addition, thinkers of an earlier epoch, with little or faulty knowledge of human biology, attributed enormous importance to the male seed. The man's semen seemed to be the exclusive potent ingredient in human procreation. This seed needed the warm, nurturing confines of a woman's womb in order to grow and develop into a human being. But in this understanding, the woman had no substantive role in procreation. Her only contribution was to nourish and protect the male seed, which was thought to hold within itself all the necessary potential for life.

The great medieval theologian Thomas Aquinas summed up this prevailing view of sexual reproduction: "When the generation is completed, *the seed itself, unchanged and fulfilled,* is the offspring which is born" (our emphasis). So self-sufficient is the male's seed that the birth of a female child signals a flaw in the process—a woman being, in Aristotle's succinct phrase, "a misbegotten male."

The almost obsessive moral concern over masturbation may have yet another root. Formal ethical reflection has been until quite recently an enterprise undertaken almost exclusively by men. Among Catholics, for example, the discipline of moral theology developed to offer guidance to priests in their ministry. Rather than a public reflection on significant social issues (as it is today), moral theology was an in-house discussion—a pastoral discipline aimed at the education of seminarians and priests. These ministers would, in turn, use this information in their pastoral activities—in their preaching, in moral instruction, and in private guidance in the confessional. The primary audience for Catholic moral teaching, then, was not the broad community of faith including women and men, both married and single persons. It was to priests and, in particular, to adolescent and young adult men studying for the priesthood, that moral theology was originally addressed. This audience of young unmarried men may well have intensified the significance of sexual self-pleasuring.

A moral theology developed by priests for priests (and then for others) leaves another legacy. This heritage did not reflect women's experience or that of married persons, and thus lost the benefit of this wider community's wisdom. When ethical deliberation neglects so much information, the adequacy of its conclusions comes into question.

These various factors had recognizable results. Apart from a catechetical prohibition heard now and then, Christians maintained a conspiracy of silence concerning masturbation. Silence reinforced the shame associated with self-stimulation, but seldom stopped the behavior. Instead, secrecy isolated people in private distress. Many Catholics bemoaned their weakness as a personal flaw: "surely I am the only one who masturbates! I must be a depraved person, a sexual deviant. Why can't I stop acting like this?" A confessor's counsel to eradicate this contemptible practice did little to promote understanding or healing.

In this atmosphere of silence, Catholics struggled toward some mature resolution. A married couple learned to take delight in mutual pleasuring that did not always lead to intercourse. A widower welcomed the mellow pleasure of this solitary solace. A vowed religious, over time, reached greater comfort with this expression of sexuality and self-intimacy. Other compromises were less healthy. A conscientious young adult, bedeviled by this habit since early adolescence, grew to fear and hate his sexuality; a midlife woman continued to be drawn to self-stimulation, but with deepening feelings of loneliness and shame.

Whatever the resolution, it remained private. When a personal compromise simply reinforced the pain, privacy made healing difficult. When a mature resolution yielded insight, this wisdom was seldom available to the wider community of faith.

The Variety of Pleasure

The mother of two small children takes a leisurely bath at the end of a hectic day. In a mood of quiet reflection, she explores her own body. Like other "good Catholic girls," she had learned as a child to remain mostly ignorant of her body and its arousals. Her lovemaking with her husband is generally good, but she still finds much in her experience of arousal and pleasure to be mysterious. Through her twenties and early thirties she has become more comfortable with bodies: her own, her husband's with its different rhythms, her children's with their fragility and loveliness. Sometimes she looks at her four-year-old daughter's body and sees her own, as if for the first time.

In the lazy comfort of her bath, she takes time to touch her body, slowly exploring its shape and feel. She is a bit embarrassed but mostly amused by the pleasure this engenders. She offers a quick prayer of thanks, grateful for the ways she is coming to know and love her body more.

Here self-pleasuring occurs in a particular context; the mood is quiet introspection, without the compulsiveness that often dominates the stereotypic masturbation of the adolescent male. The goal is self-discovery more than the quick and guilty release of sexual tension. The hope this action embodies is greater self-awareness, self-acceptance, even a deeper love of oneself. But such experiences have had little influence on typical pastoral discussions of masturbation.

A very different experience occurs in the life of the normal adolescent boy. This thirteen-year-old is regularly thrown off stride by the insistent eruptions of puberty. He is suddenly aroused by persons and images and fantasies that seem to surround him. But he remains strikingly alone in this new and confusing experience. He has no sexual partner and will not have one for some years to come. His body is suddenly matured beyond his psyche and his social self. Depending on the moral messages he has received from his environment, his experiences of self-stimulation may be enjoyable or guilt-ridden. For some adolescents these actions become compulsive: they feel driven or obsessed by physical arousal.

Most bewildering for many teenage boys is the link between sexual stimulation and control. Shame threatens the adolescent who cannot avoid having an erection at a swimming pool or in a locker room. Most often successful at control in these situations, he is less successful in private. If he understands his sexual behavior as sinful, he may pray for deliverance from this uncontrollable urge. He may even learn to hate this body that humiliates him with its urgent desires.

A different experience of pleasuring happens in lovemaking. Married for a dozen years, a couple have come to enjoy just lying close together. Sometimes their embrace leads to intercourse; often it does not. At times their mutual caresses lead to orgasm without intercourse. These experiences are so mutually satisfying that the couple has never even questioned the "moral rectitude" of this behavior. To them the word masturbation seems a crude and improper description of this part of their love play. This experience of pleasuring is an important part of lovemaking in many marriages. Couples know that it contributes to the complex fruitfulness of their love. The institutional church has been slow to acknowledge this experience of sexual pleasure in its reflection on responsible committed love.

A fourth context of self-pleasuring leads us into a tragic category of sexual release—masturbation as a compensation for loneliness and loss of control. The example here is a fifty-year-old prison inmate, now deprived of his freedom and of the daily direction of his own life. In the enforced solitude of these unnatural circumstances, he turns repeatedly to masturbation. This obsessive behavior is less about sex than about control. In a milieu devoid of affection and freedom, self-stimulation acts as a lament, a lonely grieving in which the person can experience some momentary control, some fleeting ability to be aroused, in however wounded a fashion. In his novel *The Falconer,* John Cheever provides a painful portrait of this ritual of pleasure and sorrow. This behavior bears some similarity to the adolescent's experience in its compulsiveness and loneliness. It is strikingly unlike the experience of gentle self-exploration or mutual pleasuring in lovemaking.

Theologian Rosemary Haughton discusses another example of sexual pleasuring, one that brings crisis and healing to center stage. Her essay in *Commitment to Partnership* exposes a painful yet common aspect of sexuality: sexual abuse. Drawing on her experience as the director of a women's refuge, Haughton describes one familiar route to healing. These women are fleeing domestic violence, often bringing their children with them. Usually they spend several months in the safety of this common residence. In a significant step toward recovery, two women may move out with their children and split the rent of a shared apartment. Living in this violence-free atmosphere, the women continue to heal the scars that years of sexual abuse have left. Sometimes their friendship and mutual care will include expressions of sexual affection. Tentatively, they learn that sexual contact is not necessarily violent or abusive. Slowly they relearn the loveliness of

their own bodies, the goodness of sexual pleasure. To call these healing touches "masturbation" reveals a poverty of both vocabulary and
theology.

These differing instances of sexual pleasuring invite us to reexamine our historical judgments about self-stimulation. These stories lead
us to questions of motives and meanings.

Motives and Meanings

What meanings can be discerned in these experiences? What motives
stir our own arousals? A moral code that instructs us simply to flee sexual arousal as an "occasion of sin" offers no opportunity to reflect on
these important questions. But if we are attentive to our bodies and
our behaviors, we may learn something significant about ourselves.
We may come to a better understanding of our hopes and hidden
wounds.

Traditionally, the moral meaning of self-pleasuring was captured in
the term self-abuse. For many people, this term served as a polite synonym for masturbation. In this narrowed meaning, sexual self-pleasuring was understood as a degraded form of self-inflicted injury.
Experience today points to other far more devastating ways to damage
ourselves. Alcohol is now acknowledged to affect one-third of the families in America. Whether we understand it as an illness or an addiction or a moral failing, alcoholism is an exercise in self-abuse with
profound and observable social consequences. Eating disorders—from
chronic obesity to anorexia and bulimia—are on the rise in American
society. In these exercises of self-abuse, both physical and spiritual sustenance is refused. Pain that cannot be expressed is swallowed, but this
private consumption gives no real nourishment. Cigarette smoking
may not be a "sin," but it is certainly self-abuse. Begun for enjoyment
or in an effort to find social approval, smoking becomes for many
people an almost unbreakable habit—a compulsion that leads, literally,
to the grave. Here again, the social injury from such personal abuse is
substantial.

Self-abuse remains an important moral theme. We judge an action
abusive according to its destructiveness—of the individual and of the
community. Sexual self-stimulation, *when compulsive*, may belong in
this category. Most often, however, self-pleasuring is neither abusive
nor compulsive.

Compulsion and Control

The social sciences have yet to fully understand the coded messages concealed in our compulsions. In behaviors that we perform repeatedly, unable to stop ourselves, we both conceal and reveal our distress. What are we trying to announce in compulsive acts of sexual self-stimulation? In this peculiarly human strategy we both punish ourselves and try to announce some unacknowledged pain. But to the person afflicted by compulsive behavior, the signal is seldom so clear.

One common message seems to be that our life is not flourishing. A midlife woman becomes overburdened by her work; she has no time for rest or leisure or the simple delights of friendship. A habit of compulsive self-stimulation arises or returns in her life. This behavior seems to cry out, "I am starved for affection and rest and pleasure. My life is out of control!" The message does not necessarily demand a drastic reordering of her life. But it may well signal the need for some significant change.

A previously successful minister confronts a difficult time in his career. Recently arrived in a new parish, he feels less and less effective here. None of his current efforts brings success or bears fruit. At a distance from many previous friends and colleagues, he has yet to establish here relationships of any depth. With both his relationships and work in crisis, a sense of impotence overwhelms him. A practice of compulsive self-stimulation ensues. By these actions he struggles to assert some control or find some potency in his life. His vocation is not at risk; he has not intentionally turned away from God. But his present circumstances do not sustain him.

Privatizing Pleasure

Sexual arousal is meant to move us toward other people. Our hesitant responses and tentative embraces lead us toward enduring relationships and life commitments. But this goal of fruitful contact, of genuine engagement with other people, is not realized in every arousal. Our genital arousals, social in orientation, sometimes find no social expression. This is more an anomaly than an unnatural act. Self-stimulation does not, of itself, make us perverted or unclean or sinful.

Trouble arises when self-stimulation becomes a person's *ordinary style* of sexual expression. When this behavior becomes habitual, in ways that replace our genuine, sustained contact with other people, then there is reason to be concerned. But, as John Perito reminds us, even most adolescent masturbation should not be seen simply as isolating behavior, since the fantasies that accompany these actions are more often "preparation for the foreplay and intercourse of later life."

The danger of genital self-pleasuring becoming a dead end instead of a passage to sexual maturity remains real for young men in American culture today. Unsure of himself with women, a young man may slip into a habit of self-stimulation while enjoying fantasies of "the ideal woman." This romantic fantasy is, of course, insistently fueled by much in media advertising and by a pornography industry that profitably markets sexual illusions. The fantasies of voluptuous, passive, and willing women are not so much "dirty" as they are distorted. These images, which regularly crowd the pages of men's magazines, depict women as extraordinarily beautiful and wonderfully docile. They do not talk back. They do not make demands. At the same time, they display no physical limitation or personality flaw. What a charming world! Its only deficiency is its falseness.

A man who lingers too long in such a fantasy realm (a natural rest stop for the confused adolescent on the way to adulthood) will have trouble with the women who populate his real world of work and friendship. The demands made by actual women will confuse him. Their strengths and weaknesses will trouble or offend him. Bewildered by the differences between his inner and outer worlds, he may choose to retreat to a safer, more controllable domain. Here he can find pleasure without interpersonal risk. This lifestyle can become as self-abusive as that of the alcoholic. The pleasure is private but the damage is social. He is unprepared for the ordinary dynamics of negotiation and compromise that arise in daily interactions with real women. His private life—where his sexuality enjoys unrestricted expression—has not readied him for these challenges. Missed expectations, false demands, and failed commitments: these become the bitter fruit of a behavior that had initially seemed private and harmless.

Significant, Not Sinful

When we touch ourselves to bring about orgasm, we do something significant. Our sexuality is too important a part of our life to describe this simply as a release of physiological tension. As a growing number of theologians have judged, we rarely sin in doing this, though we may abuse ourselves when the dynamics of compulsion and punishment replace genuine pleasure. Whatever the motive or meaning, we are doing something significant.

Shared with a lover or spouse, sex play can express affection and care. Self-pleasuring may, in a very different context, reveal an adolescent fantasy of being totally in control. Recognizing this may be the first step of the journey from a self-centered, adolescent sexuality to a maturity that makes responsible sexual sharing possible. The revelations in our sexual lives are varied and often well disguised. But they *are* revelations, and we need to pay attention to them.

We open ourselves to important information by not turning away from our sexual experience, by learning to trust the insight we gain in our sexual lives. We also open ourselves by changing our vocabulary and our descriptions of these most personal activities. For many people, the term *masturbation* carries too many negative nuances to be useful; perhaps the time has come to retire this word. Self-stimulation and self-pleasuring may be more useful notions. None of these words, however, captures the fruitful sharing of genital pleasure, apart from intercourse, that many devoted couples enjoy. A more honest discussion in the community of faith may generate a better vocabulary for our sexual lives.

Finally, Christian discussions of sexual morality always seem to come back to the "tyranny of the ideal." In Jesus of Nazareth we are given an example of a uniquely generous and fruitful life. His is a life of great paradox: brief, but enormously effective; childless, but profoundly fruitful. Jesus' life offers us high ideals while dictating few particular life choices. Through the historical development of our religious tradition, each generation of Christians draws out the implications of Jesus' life for its own time.

Rules and restrictions multiplied in Christianity as our ancestors sought to illumine the path of following Christ. One unfortunate dynamic in this religious history has been the tendency to transform ideals into laws. The gospel ideal of a lifelong marriage became the law of indissolubility—a Christian marriage *cannot* end. The ideal of having community leaders who are single-minded and lead exemplary lives became the law of clerical celibacy. When freedom and generosity, so abundantly available in the life of Jesus, give way to strict observance and rectitude—this is the tyranny of the ideal.

The ideal concerning our genital arousals is clear. These pleasurable stirrings ideally lead us toward a partner, a committed life companion. With this partner sexual pleasure becomes mutual delight, bearing fruit in children and a deepening relationship. In such a relationship, we learn the rhythms and disciplines of receiving and giving pleasure. Such is the ideal. Life, however, has a more complex texture. Not every vocation includes a life partner: death and divorce deprive us of sexual companions; mature decisions move us toward a single or celibate lifestyle; all of us journey through adolescence—that strange land where we are biologically fit but psychologically unready for the responsibilities of sexual sharing.

We have been taught that to actively experience genital pleasure in these latter contexts is shameful and wrong. Such pleasuring is so sinful that it removes us from life with God. Here the tyranny of the ideal joins forces with a suspicion of sexuality. This merger binds and bewilders many Christians. Today fewer Christians accept without question formal religious teachings regarding sexuality. The tyranny and suspicion revealed in many official statements are too deeply at odds with the life of Jesus to be believable. Trusting their own experience as it is purified by decades of faithful religious living, more and more Christians are ready to participate in the necessary healing of the churches' understanding of sexuality and genital pleasure.

Our responsibility as Christians will always be to make our sexual lives generous instead of selfish; fruitful rather than manipulative. Our responsibility is also to speak the truth we recognize as our experiences of sex, sexuality, and intimacy mature. In such courageous and candid conversations, we will be revealed to ourselves, and we will more richly honor the mysterious rhythms of love in human life.

REFLECTIVE EXERCISE

We all have experienced the inclination toward sexual self-stimulation. It can be useful to reflect on the circumstances of this arousal in our own lives, respectful of the information about our sexual self that we may find there.

Are there particular times or situations in your life (fatigue or loneliness or curiosity or disappointment) that have moved you toward self-stimulation? What thoughts or feelings or moods have been part of these situations? Do you find a pattern here?

Has your attitude or behavior regarding self-pleasuring undergone change? If so, what factors have influenced the change?

ADDITIONAL RESOURCES

The 1976 report of the Catholic Theological Society of America marked an important turning point in Catholic understanding and pastoral practice; its discussion of masturbation remains helpful. See Anthony Kosnik et al., *Human Sexuality: New Directions in American Catholic Thought.* John Perito provides an updated discussion of genital self-pleasuring in his *Sexuality and Faith: A Psychiatric Approach;* see also James McCary's *Human Sexuality.*

Theologian Charles Curran gives a brief and clear analysis of the views that shaped the traditional Catholic view of masturbation in his *Themes in Fundamental Moral Theology.* John Mahoney's helpful historical overview is found in *The Making of Moral Theology.* Vincent Genovesi provides a summary and critique of the current discussion of masturbation among Catholic moralists; see *In Pursuit of Love: Catholic Morality and Human Sexuality.*

Thomas Aquinas's observation on reproduction is found in *Summa Contra Gentiles* IV, 45. For a clear exploration of Aquinas's view of sexuality see Chapter 6 of Lisa Sowle Cahill's *Between the Sexes.* Morton and Barbara Kelsey offer useful observations on self-stimulation in their *Sacrament of Sexuality.* Rosemary Haughton's essay "The Meaning of Marriage in Women's New Consciousness" appears in *Commitment to Partnership,* edited by William Roberts.

Conclusion

Caritas—Love Realized and Transformed

No one has seen God, but as long as we love one another God will live in us and God's love will be complete in us. (1 John 4:12)

SEX, SEXUALITY, INTIMACY—in each of these we meet the human ambition for love. Rooted in our bodies—in the delights and needs that draw us toward one another—love leads us beyond ourselves. Love can even lead us to God. Christians celebrate love as the beginning and end of our religious tradition. Creation itself is a gift of God's affection. The Creator "so loved the world" that Jesus was sent among us. Love becomes the great commandment for Jews and Christians: "You must love the Lord, your God, with all your heart, with all your soul, with all your strength, and with all your mind, and your neighbor as yourself" (Luke 10:27; Jesus is quoting Deuteronomy 6:5). Love is to be the identifying characteristic of those who follow the way of Jesus: "By this love that you have for one another, everyone will know that you are my disciples" (John 13:35).

The love that Jesus lived and taught has long been described by Christians as *caritas*—charity. Those who attempt to follow Jesus today, aware that love is central, recognize that religious rhetoric often robs the word *charity* of much of its force. Charity then degenerates into a sentimental "feeling kindly toward others," a bland virtue exercised in the facile enjoinder to "have a nice day." The robust challenges of *caritas*—urging us to effective action in social and political areas and compelling us to love strangers and enemies as our own—are lost in a piety that asks too little of us.

"Our love is not to be just words or mere talk, but something real and active" (1 John 3:18). Genuine love moves beyond rhetoric and sentiment. Charity must carry love through from arousal to action. *Caritas* shapes the affections of *eros* into generous care. As a virtue, charity becomes habitual—a resident strength that guides our love into consistent and effective behavior. Charity gives love endurance and sustains our hope to be faithful and fruitful. Among Christians, charity encompasses not only the affection we feel for our closest friends but also the actions by which we support the well-being of those who are not "our kind."

As we search for this hardier virtue of charity, we need to track the maturing of love. Love often begins in romance and erotic arousal. Strong feelings of affection accompany the attraction we feel for one another. We rejoice in the physical delights of love.

Eros, which begins in the body, becomes the enemy of *caritas* only when it stops there. Eros fails us if we equate loveliness with physical beauty or sexual prowess alone. When the body is love's only abode, change becomes an enemy. Fidelity is foolish; commitment a trap.

As love matures, eros moves toward a more profound and enduring bond. Erotic love expands beyond a narrow sexual focus to thrive on broader expression—the intimate exchanges of affection and concern that only time together can teach. This love sustains a relationship through a long period of absence or illness. Despite the loss of genital expression or even a lack of accustomed mutuality, the bond survives and affection flourishes. We see this strength today: a spouse succumbs to Alzheimer's disease; a lover is stricken with AIDS. Erotic excitement subsides but love endures. The partner continues the daily deeds of love—presence, patience, faithful care—not from guilt but from affection. Such intimacy is, most emphatically, not romantic. The emotion that sustains intimacy here is not sexual passion but the deeper bond of devotion.

Not all intimate relationships require this kind of commitment. Nor is such dramatic devotion always possible. But when we witness such fidelity, we are—all of us—reminded of the possibilities of love. Eros, begun in physical arousal and expressed in sexual delight, has been transformed in love. Devotion develops not by repudiating eros but by expanding its expression and deepening its bonds.

Charity accompanies friendship and delight, as part of our affection for one another. But *caritas* carries us beyond mutuality, enabling us to love the unfamiliar face of the stranger and the battered body of the wounded. This love, neither rooted in sexual arousal nor fulfilled in genital sharing, is both natural and more than natural: To love these others as our sisters and brothers is to be truly human, and yet the ability to do so makes us most exceptional.

Christian love is not a wholly different love. We are not called to love in an entirely unique fashion but to exercise the extraordinary capacity for love that we find within ourselves. The vision and values that excite us to such love stamp this maturation as Christian. Stories of the generous love of saints and prophets, missionaries and martyrs, fill our rich religious tradition. These models show us that courageous love is possible and strengthen us to act this way ourselves.

What does it mean to call this vision Christian? That life has a purpose that goes beyond ourselves alone, that "others" are more like us than different, that commitment and fidelity are possible—this vision illuminates several religious traditions. These are *Christian* insights because, for us, God has revealed these possibilities through the life of Jesus Christ. His way of living changes us, making us see life differently.

The Christian Gospels confront us with the witness of Jesus. His behavior argues that personal commitment and vulnerability are worth the risk. His life challenges the cultural biases that make self-preservation and "getting my fair share" our central goals. Giving our life for other people, learning to forgive and to accept forgiveness, using our resources to make the future better—we begin to see these as possible and worthy goals.

This way of seeing marks the beginning of religious faith. Christianity carries a special vision of the world, revealing to us who we are and who we might be. But this vision sometimes seems evanescent. Its insights come and go; they do not always seem defensible. On certain days the evidence against this vision overwhelms us. We lose the point of our own life, or we are injured by someone we love, or confused by the senseless violence in the world. We become painfully aware that we are not the source of the vision; it comes instead as a gift. And when the vision comes, it arouses us to live differently. This vision of *caritas* invites the transformation of eros. Christians have traditionally called this vision-as-gift by the name of faith. Faith comes as a gift with strings attached, for the vision compels us to act in new ways. Like charity, faith is not a private sentiment but a commitment to action. Our religious faith becomes practical in our effort to live, in a daily and concrete fashion, what we have received.

Christianity celebrates a deeper meaning of love that is easily lost or obscured in the hectic pace of life. Our religious heritage carries an insight, a vision into what is ordinarily invisible—the power and presence all around us of God's redeeming love for the world. *Caritas* connects us to that graceful vision. In our own actions of mercy and love we participate in the transforming power of *caritas*. The transformation of our love, which finds expression in care and forgiveness, carries us beyond ourselves in kinship and concern for the future.

Care

> Love is always patient and kind; it is never jealous; love is never boastful or conceited; it is never rude or selfish; it does not take offense, and is not resentful. Love takes no pleasure in other people's sins but delights in truth. It is always ready to excuse, to trust, to hope, and to endure whatever comes. (1 Corinthians 13:4–7)

Caritas expands in care, both fulfilling and transforming love. Care is an active concern for the well-being of those we love, not just as extensions of us but for themselves. The capacity to care includes both power and nurturance. In this expansion of love, some of us struggle to learn how to nurture others. Some men, socialized to see themselves solely as makers and doers in their own right, find nurturance difficult. Learning to care—to invest our self in other people's lives in ways that respond to their genuine needs—comes as a challenge. Many men welcome the challenge, recognizing that it opens them to a new world of affection and mutual concern. But other men find nurturance too difficult or too threatening or just too time consuming. However, without the expansion of self that comes from nurturing other people, this kind of man can approach midlife with an uneasy sense of stagnation or loss. An aggressive self-starter in his thirties, in his fifties he takes on the defended rigidity of the "self-made man."

For women the challenge can be different. Trained since childhood to discern and respond to the needs of others, many women find that nurturing comes easily. But personal power remains alien. One woman notes, "I have never really thought of myself as powerful. I don't feel particularly competent or independent or strong. In fact, I feel that I don't have much direct involvement in life. I can take care of people—my children, my husband—and I think I do that pretty well.

But I have little sense that I make any direct contribution of my own to the world. Sometimes I feel like an empty shell."

For a woman, learning to care well can mean developing a richer sense of her personal power. Without this self-awareness and the confidence that comes with it, the nurturing woman can feel unfocused, insubstantial, "like an empty shell." Her care can disintegrate into anxiety or harden into a meddling concern. The capacity to care is rooted in an awareness of personal power. It is this power that we use, we spend, we give away as we care for others. If we see our self as having no power, our efforts to care are continually imperiled: either we burn out trying to please others or we keep others dependent on us, so that we can feel strong.

But this is not *caritas*. Charity nurtures life, not continued dependency. To care is to use our power to support another's growth. To love well is to know how to come close to other people in ways that give life. To love well may also mean to learn how to let go.

Learning to let go in love—this is the special discipline at the heart of *caritas*. Care is purified as it expands beyond control. When we cannot "have it our way," when our relationship no longer develops according to our plan, can we still love? Can we continue to invest our self in the well-being of others, when their lives take a direction that goes beyond what we think is best for them? Love remains untested until we experience the demand to love others, not just for what they bring to our life but for themselves. Surviving this test, love is transformed.

Love expands as we learn to care with less control. Care ushers us into the maturity of stewardship. As stewards we are responsible for others without possessing them. When we are tempted to hold on too tightly, *caritas* reminds us that all love comes to us as gift.

Forgiveness

> If your brother does something wrong, reprove him and, if he is sorry, forgive him. And if he wrongs you seven times a day and seven times comes back to you and says, "I am sorry," you must forgive him. (Luke 17:3-4)

One of the actions most emphasized by Jesus and most enjoined upon his followers is forgiveness. Forgiveness expands love. In forgiving, we *choose* not to let the hurt we have experienced get in the way of this relationship continuing. Forgiveness enables us to start again, to come to a sense of a new beginning.

Forgiving involves a decision that is not completed in the moment of choice. As a process, forgiveness gradually allows the hurt to heal and the trust between us to be renewed. The process of forgiving does not bring us back to where we were. Nor does it allow us to go on as if nothing has happened. Something *has* happened, something profound. The fabric of our interwoven lives has been torn. We can neither forget this nor deny it. Yet we can choose not to be defined by this rupture. Instead we can incorporate it as part of an ongoing relationship. We hope that the hurt we have experienced will not become the pattern, but we sense its contribution of depth and substance to our interaction.

Neither extending nor receiving forgiveness is easy. In order to forgive we must experience our pain and face the offense that is its cause. We must be willing to test our hurt to determine if our feelings of anger are justified. If we submit our feelings to this kind of scrutiny, we may find that we are wrong. We may find that we have misjudged another's motives or overreacted to an event. But, rather than acknowledging this mistake, we may prefer to nurse the anger and refuse to consider forgiveness.

The self-examination that forgiveness requires shows us ways in which we have contributed to the hurt. In few situations is one party solely to blame; most interactions are conjoint, with each of us contributing to the problems that develop. But, again, seeing our self as the innocent victim may be more important to us than risking the self-knowledge that forgiveness demands.

Genuine forgiveness also robs us of our hurt. We can no longer harbor it for later use against the other person. We must surrender the wound or injustice that may have become a cherished, if bitter, possession. Letting go of this vengeful possession, we lose a painful advantage we have been savoring, but we regain the personal energy that has been dissipated as we nourished this hurt. In a sense, forgiveness evens the score, for it undercuts the sense that we have something to hold over the other person. In forgiving, we start out anew, perhaps humbled (we know how fragile a relationship can be) but hopeful too.

Forgiveness is both hard to give and difficult to receive. To accept forgiveness we must revisit the pain we have caused. We have to acknowledge our responsibility; we may even have to admit that we were wrong. Here again, we may find that denying all this is easier than reaching out in love. To need forgiveness is humbling. As long as we are in the right, we have no such need. To accept forgiveness is to acknowledge our guilt—not only to our self but to the other person as well.

But, while difficult, forgiveness is often the only path to peace. At times we cannot talk enough or explain enough or regret enough to bring the two of us back together. The harm has been too heavy; the distance between us is now too great to bridge. In these situations we relearn that forgiveness is more than a personal achievement; it is a gift and a grace that, spent by our anger, we must await in hope.

The promise of forgiveness is one of the most startling of Christian hopes. We discover that we have the power to change the past! After a severe injury, our hearts tend to harden. Or after a failure of love, we stoically shrug: "It happened; nothing can be done." The Gospels reveal another way. We can forgive—even ancient wounds and absent persons. *Caritas* prompts us to expect the extraordinary even from ourselves. In the strength of love, we contradict the power of the past and the force of its failures. We can forgive what has been done to us—by parents, by adversaries, by institutions.

In Jesus' life forgiveness takes on an importance that even his followers found difficult to accept. Overturning the religious wisdom of his day, Jesus insisted that virtue is found less in an upright observance of the law than in forgiving one another. A woman caught in adultery is brought into a public square to be shamed and even stoned. Jesus seems uninterested in punishment. His care for the woman suggests the three elements of reconciliation: acknowledging the wrong, letting it go, and changing our life to turn away from future wrongdoing. Jesus did not invent forgiveness, but he refined the shape of this power and announced that it was available to all. And Jesus made this virtue an identifying characteristic of those who would follow him. We, too, must be willing to forgive—our enemies, our friends, even ourselves.

Forgiveness is a face of charity. This virtue alters the nature of Christian community, inviting us to see ourselves as a gathering of the wounded and sinful, not just the virtuous or chosen. Such a community carries an extraordinary resource—the power to forgive. The Christian community thus becomes a place of reconciliation.

Kinship

> Lord, when did we see you hungry and feed you, or thirsty and give you drink? When did we see you a stranger and make you welcome, naked and clothe you or in prison and go to see you? And the king will answer, "I tell you solemnly, in so far as you did this to one of the least of these siblings of mine, you did it to me." (Matthew 25:39)

Caritas impels a third transformation of love. Intimacy expands when we glimpse the hidden kinship among us. Jesus, echoing the prophets before him, repeatedly calls us to this vision: the poor, the orphan, the outcast are not just outsiders to be pitied or ignored. They belong to our family; they are one of us. Influenced by this vision, Christians begin to see others not as aliens and strangers but as our sisters and brothers. The walls that defend family and neighborhood and faith from "those others" begin to fall away. With the eyes of faith, we see that the stranger is the neighbor and the neighbor is Christ. We see that even the enemy is "our kind."

In this privileged moment, as we are given insight into human community, love expands. We belong to one another; we have a stake in each other's lives. *Caritas* calls us to this conviction. The "others" who make up the world—whether these are the homeless or people living with disabilities, undocumented workers or political refugees—are more like us than they are different. Putting aside the defenses that protect us from those of a different color or custom or economic class, we see their similarity to us. This peculiar and surprising insight, which flies in the face of much of our socialization, invites us to care for those others with mercy and justice.

Basic to the Christian vision is the conviction that we are for more than ourselves. The call of Jesus reinforces this invitation to generous love. "If a person who was rich in this world's goods saw that one of his brothers was in need, but closed his heart to him, how could the love of God be living in him?" (1 John 3:17). Christian faith expands the boundaries of our concern. Our care includes whoever is in need. Charity presses against the walls that protect our private property. We find that we belong to a larger family. Our resources are not just our possessions; they are the means of our contribution to a world that is more just.

The issues of justice and social action that we face in our own lives are complex. In many questions, the "right answer" does not emerge quickly or without doubt; persons of good will and wisdom come to different conclusions about what should be done. When the issues at stake touch directly on our own lives or our family's welfare—as in questions of job security or tax reform or national defense—determining the just response is even more difficult.

In these situations Christian awareness gives no easy answers, but it does give us a starting point. We are not for ourselves alone. *Others* are not strangers but siblings. As Pope Paul VI proclaimed, action for justice and the transformation of the world are at the heart of our response to the gospel. The gospel challenges us to share the burdens of humankind and to participate in its liberation. The ways in which we participate in this mission of Jesus will differ among us. But we can expect that our own maturing as Christians will include this larger mission of *caritas*, to which the words and witness of Jesus call us.

Fruitfulness for the Future

As a branch cannot bear fruit all by itself, but must remain part of the vine, neither can you unless you remain in me. I am the vine and you are the branches. (John 15:4)

Love that does not serve life will die: *caritas* calls us to this truth. Real mutuality is fruitful. The desire to create something together is close to the heart of intimacy—whether expressed in genital love or in collaborative work. A relationship that does not nurture this impulse risks stagnation. An unfruitful love will not thrive.

Psychologists are aware of the significance of this creative impulse. They warn that when we do not move beyond ourselves, we imperil a love relationship. A "pseudo-intimacy" can result, turning the partners in upon themselves in a way that gradually impoverishes the relationship. The result of this failure to expand our concern is not an intimacy more protected and complete, but stagnation. Having failed to share our love beyond ourselves we soon find that we have little left to give each other.

Our religious tradition has always cherished this truth: love is not a private affair. *Caritas*, which moves us beyond ourselves, even beyond "our kind," opens us to the future. In love, we generate the future. Our children, whom we have created in our love, belong to the future more than they do to us. This is true in other creative activity as well.

Our projects, our plans, our productive work contribute to a world that goes beyond our own life span. Our creativity links us to the future. But the future always escapes us, for it is necessarily beyond our control.

Love invites us to pour out our power in creativity and care. But the invitation entails considerable risk. To be creative we must be willing to give our power to the future. This concern for the future is a movement of self-transcendence. The impulse to go beyond our self may be fragile; it may even fail under pressure. But this urge may also develop strength, becoming part of the way we understand our relationship to the world. Our power, our resources, are for more than just ourselves. They are, in fact, for more than that broader circle of intimates who are our family. We can give our self to the future, a future we cannot fully control, a future we may not even live long enough to share.

To invest our self in a future that we may not live to see, we must believe that our self-giving will bear fruit beyond ourselves. For Christians, this conviction is deeply grounded in faith, faith that the future belongs to God.

Our model here, once again, is Jesus. His life offers us a paradox of fruitful love: childless, he generated all those of us who name ourselves Christians. Calling humankind to a new way of being with God and one another, he gathered around him in love a group of followers to whom he would entrust the future of his mission. His prayer over Jerusalem, uttered as his own life was coming—prematurely—to an end, displayed his frustration and concern: "How often have I longed to gather your children, as a hen gathers her chicks under her wings, and you refused!" (Matthew 23:37). The night before his death Jesus struggled to understand the unexpected direction his life was taking; he labored to accept a more mysterious design for his contribution to those he loves. He rebelled against the loss of his own dreams and ambitions and begged for a different future: "'Father,' he said, 'if you are willing, take this cup away from me'" (Luke 22:42). Surely now was not the time to let go of his own power and plan. His mission had barely begun, his followers were scarcely ready to carry on without him. Only in great turmoil and the anguish of a bloody sweat did Jesus come to accept this letting go of his life as part of his generative love.

As Christians, we are a people who struggle to let Jesus' life shape our own. So we, following him, give ourselves to the future in the faith that God will see it through, blessing and healing what we have generated in our love and what we must—in love—soon relinquish.

REFLECTIVE EXERCISE

The Gospels abound in the stories and parables of Jesus. These images, deep in our consciousness, express most powerfully the convictions and hopes we hold for our own lives. Return to a Gospel image that is important to you. What parable or event or saying comes to you as an image of the love that Jesus proclaims?

Let the memories come as they will. There is no need to force a response; wait for an image that holds power for you now. When an image arises, spend time with it. Be attentive—let it disclose its meaning to you. After some time, consider these questions:

- In what ways does this Gospel image strengthen and support your understanding of *caritas*?

- How does this Gospel image challenge your understanding of *caritas*?

- What practical response does this Gospel vision of love ask of you these days?

ADDITIONAL RESOURCES

Biblical scholar Pheme Perkins examines the words and witness of Jesus in *Love Commands in the New Testament.* Religious psychologist Jack Dominian explores the dynamics of charity in spiritual growth in *The Capacity to Love.* Marie Fortune links love and sexual ethics in *Love Does No Harm.*

Judy Logue offers a practical account of the dynamics of forgiveness in *Forgiving the People You Love to Hate.* In *Forgiveness: Finding Freedom through Reconciliation,* Avis Clendenen and Troy Martin develop a biblically based and pastorally effective model of the forgiveness exchange. Robert Schreiter examines the broad scope of forgiveness in *The Ministry of Reconciliation: Spirituality and Strategies.* For further discussion of the theological and pastoral dimensions of forgiveness, see William Countryman, *Forgiven and Forgiving;* L. Gregory Jones, *Embodying Forgiveness;* and Geiko Muller-Fahrenholz, *The Art of Forgiveness.*

In *Virtues for Ordinary Christians,* James Keenan discusses charity as the source of Christian living, "the very presence of God in our lives."

G. Simon Harak explores charity as "a passion for justice"; see his *Virtuous Passions: The Formation of Christian Character.* Jewish philosopher Emmanuel Levinas emphasizes our response to the "other" as the basis of our full humanity; his writings are increasingly influential in Christian theological and ethical thought. For a brief introduction, see George Kunz, *The Paradox of Power and Weakness.*

Social psychologist Alice Rossi connects care and social responsibility in *Caring and Doing for Others.* Erik Erikson's discussions of generative care are classic in the psychology of adulthood; for a comprehensive exploration of generativity, see John Kotre, *Outliving the Self* and *Making It Count: How to Generate a Legacy that Gives Meaning to Your Life,* and the important collection of essays in *Generativity and Adult Development,* edited by Dan McAdams and Edward de St. Aubin. We draw on Erikson's theory in our discussion of religious generativity in Chapter 5 of *Christian Life Patterns* and Chapter 4 of *Seasons of Strength.*

Bibliography

Abbott, Walter M., ed. "The Constitution on the Church" (*Lumen Gentium*). In *The Documents of Vatican II.* New York: America Press, 1966.

Anderson. Herbert. "Men and Grief." In *The Care of Men,* edited by Christie Cozad Neuger and James Newton Poling. Nashville: Abingdon, 1997.

———, and Freda Gardner. *Living Alone.* Louisville, Ky.: Westminster John Knox, 1997.

Angier, Natalie. *Woman: An Intimate Geography.* New York: Anchor Books, 2000.

Aries, Elizabeth. *Men and Women in Interaction: Reconsidering the Differences.* New York: Oxford University Press, 1996.

Barton, Marjorie. *Living Single in a Double World.* New York: Sterling House, 1999.

Baruch, Grace, Rosalind Barnett, and Caryl Rivers. *Life Prints: New Patterns of Love and Work for Today's Women.* New York: New American Library, 1983.

Bawer, Bruce. *A Place at the Table: The Gay Individual in American Society.* New York: Touchstone Books, 1994.

Bennett, Joel. *Time and Intimacy: A New Science of Personal Relationships.* Mahwah, N.J.: Lawrence Erlbaum, 2000.

Bloch, Ariel, and Chana Bloch, eds. *The Song of Songs.* Los Angeles: University of California Press, 1998.

Bly, Robert. *Iron John: A Book about Men.* New York: Vintage, 1992.

Bonsor, Jack. "Homosexual Orientation and Anthropology: Reflections on the Category 'Objective Disorder.'" *Theological Studies* 56 (1998).

Brooten, Bernadette. *Love Between Women: Early Christian Responses to Female Homoeroticism.* Chicago: University of Chicago Press, 1998.

Brown, Peter. *The Body and Society: Men, Women, and Sexual Renunciation in Early Christianity.* New York: Columbia University Press, 1988.

Brown, Wayne. *Living the Renewed Life.* New York: Golden Books, 1999.

Cahill, Lisa Sowle. *Between the Sexes: Foundations of a Christian Ethics of Sexuality.* New York: Paulist Press, 1985.

———. *Sex, Gender and Christian Ethics.* New York: Cambridge University Press, 1996.

———. *Women and Sexuality.* New York: Paulist Press, 1992.

Callahan, Sidney. "Why I Changed My Mind: Thinking about Gay Marriage." *Commonweal* (April 22, 1994).

Carmody, John. *Toward a Male Spirituality.* Mystic, Conn.: Twenty-Third Publications, 1989.

"Celibacy." *The Way Supplement* No. 77 [London] 1993.

Chittister, Joan. *The Fire in These Ashes: A Spirituality of Contemporary Religious Life.* Milwaukee: Theological Book Service, 1995.

Chodorow, Nancy. *The Power of Feelings: Personal Meaning in Psychoanalysis, Gender and Culture.* New Haven, Conn.: Yale University Press, 1999.

———. *The Reproduction of Mothering: Psychoanalysis and the Sociology of Gender.* Los Angeles: University of California Press, 1999.

Clendenen, Avis, and Troy Martin. *Forgiveness: Finding Freedom Through Reconciliation.* New York: Crossroad, 2001.

Cohler, Bertram J., and Robert Galatzer-Levy. *The Course of Gay and Lesbian Lives.* Chicago: University of Chicago Press, 2000.

Coleman, Gerald. *Homosexuality: Catholic Teaching and Pastoral Practice.* New York: Paulist Press, 1996.

Collins, Raymond. *Sexual Ethics and the New Testament.* New York: Crossroad, 2000.

Conn, Joann Wolski. *Women's Spirituality: Resources for Christian Development.* 2nd edition. New York: Paulist Press, 1996.

Countryman, William. *Forgiven and Forgiving.* Harrisburg, Pa.: Morehouse Publishing, 1998.

Cozzens, Donald. *The Changing Face of the Priesthood.* Collegeville, Minn.: Liturgical Press, 2000.

Crosby, Michael. *Celibacy: Means of Control or Mandate of the Heart?* Notre Dame, Ind.: Ave Maria Press, 1996.

Curran, Charles. *Themes in Fundamental Moral Theology.* Notre Dame, Ind.: University of Notre Dame Press, 1977.

D'Augelli, Anthony, and Charlotte Patterson, eds. *Lesbian, Gay and Bisexual Identities over the Lifespan.* New York: Oxford University Press, 1996.

Davis, Phyllis. *The Power of Touch.* New York: Hay House, 1999.

Dominian, Jack. *The Capacity to Love.* New York: Paulist Press, 1985.

———. *Let's Make Love.* London: Darton, Longman & Todd, 2001.

Dowrick, Stephanie. *Intimacy and Solitude: Balancing Closeness and Independence.* New York: Norton, 1994.

Driver, Tom. "Speaking from the Body." In *Theology and the Body,* edited by John Fenton. Philadelphia: Westminster, 1974.

Dryer, Elizabeth. *Earth Crammed with Heaven: A Spirituality of Everyday Life.* New York: Paulist Press, 1994.

Durkin, Mary. *Feast of Love: Pope John Paul II on Human Intimacy.* Chicago: Loyola University Press, 1984.

Empereur, James L. *Spiritual Direction and the Gay Person.* New York: Continuum, 1999.

Erikson, Erik H. *The Erik Erikson Reader,* edited by Robert Coles. New York: Norton, 2001.

———, and Joan Mowat Erikson. *The Life Cycle Completed: A Review.* New York: Norton, 1998.

———, Joan Erikson, and Helen Kivnick. *Vital Involvement in Old Age.* New York: Norton, 1994.

Farley, Margaret. *Just Love.* New York: Continuum, 2001.

———. *Personal Commitments: Beginning, Keeping, Changing.* San Francisco: Harper, 1983.

Ferder, Fran, and John Heagle. *Your Sexual Self: Pathways to Authentic Intimacy.* Notre Dame, Ind.: Ave Maria Press, 1992.

Fiand, Barbara. *Refocusing the Vision: Religious Life into the Future.* New York: Crossroad, 2001.

Filene, Peter. *Him/Her/Self: Gender Identities in Modern America.* 3rd edition. Baltimore: Johns Hopkins University Press, 1998.

Finch, Mary Ann. *Care Through Touch: Massage as the Art of Anointing.* New York: Continuum, 2000.

Firestone, Robert, and Joyce Catlett. *Fear of Intimacy.* Washington, D.C.: American Psychological Association, 1999.

Fischer, Kathleen. *Autumn Gospel: Women in the Second Half of Life.* New York: Paulist Press, 1995.

———. *Transforming Fire: Women Using Anger Creatively.* New York: Paulist Press, 1999.

———. *Women at the Well: Feminist Perspectives on Spiritual Direction.* New York: Paulist Press, 1988.

Fischer, Kathleen, and Thomas Hart. *Promises to Keep: Developing the Skills of Marriage.* New York: Paulist Press, 1991.

Flynn, Eileen. "Responding to the 'Gay Agenda.'" *America* (September 30, 2000).

Forsyth, Sondra, and Carol Gilligan. *Girls Seen and Heard: 52 Life Lessons for Our Daughters.* New York: Tarcher, 1998.

Fortune, Marie. *Love Does No Harm: Sexual Ethics for the Rest of Us.* New York: Continuum, 2000.

Fox, Thomas C. *Sexuality and Catholicism.* New York: George Braziller, 2000.

Gaillardetz, Richard. *Perilous Vows: Marital Spirituality and the Domestic Church.* New York: Crossroad, 2002.

Geary, David C. *Male and Female: The Evolution of Human Sex Differences.* Washington, D.C.: American Psychological Association, 1998.

Genovesi, Vincent. *In Pursuit of Love: Catholic Morality and Human Sexuality.* Collegeville, Minn.: Michael Glazier, 1996.

Gilligan, Carol. *In a Different Voice: Psychological Theory and Women's Development.* With new Preface by author. Cambridge, Mass.: Harvard University Press, 1993.

Goergen, Donald. *The Sexual Celibate.* Garden City, N.Y.: Doubleday Image, 1979.

Goodman, Ellen, and Patricia O'Brien. *I Know Just What You Mean.* New York: Simon & Schuster, 2000.

Gottman, John. *Why Marriages Succeed or Fail.* New York: Simon & Schuster, 1994.

Greeley, Andrew. *Sex: The Catholic Experience.* Chicago: Thomas More Press, 1994.

Gurian, Michael. *A Fine Young Man: What Parents, Mentors, Educators Can Do to Shape Adolescent Boys into Exceptional Men.* New York: Tarcher, 1999.

———. *The Good Son: Shaping the Moral Development of Our Boys and Young Men.* New York: Tarcher, 2000.

Harak, G. Simon. *Virtuous Passions: The Formation of Christian Character.* New York: Paulist Press, 1993.

Harris, Maria. *Dance of the Spirit: The Seven Steps of Women's Spirituality.* New York: Bantam Books, 1991.

———. *Jubilee Time: Celebrating Women, Spirit and the Advent of Age.* New York: Bantam Books, 1996.

Harter, Susan. *The Construction of the Self: A Developmental Perspective.* New York: Guilford Press, 1999.

Haughton, Rosemary. "The Meaning of Marriage in Women's New Consciousness." In *Commitment to Partnership,* edited by William Roberts. New York: Paulist Press, 1987.

Hsu, Albert. *Singles at the Crossroads: A Fresh Perspective on Christian Singleness.* Chicago: InterVarsity Press, 1997.

Hunt, Mary. *A Fierce Tenderness: A Feminist Theology of Friendship.* New York: Crossroad, 1991.

Jaycox, Victoria. *Single Again: A Guide for Women Starting Over.* New York: Norton, 1998.

Johnson, Luke Timothy. "A Disembodied 'Theology of the Body.'" *Commonweal* (January 26, 2001).

Johnson, Norine, Michael Roberts, and Judith Worrell, eds. *Beyond Appearances: A New Look at Adolescent Girls.* Washington, D.C.: American Psychological Association, 1999.

Jones, L. Gregory. *Embodying Forgiveness: A Theological Analysis.* Grand Rapids, Mich.: Eerdmans, 1995.

Josselson, Ruthellen. *Finding Herself: Pathways to Identity Development in Women.* San Francisco: Jossey-Bass, 1987.

————. *Revising Herself: The Story of Women's Identity from College to Midlife.* New York: Oxford University Press, 1998.

————. *The Space Between Us: Exploring the Dimensions of Human Relationships.* New York: Sage Publishers, 1995.

Jung, Patricia Beattie, with Joseph Coray, eds. *Sexual Diversity and Catholicism: Toward the Development of Moral Theology.* Collegeville, Minn.: Liturgical Press, 2001.

Kaschak, Ellyn. *Engendered Lives: A New Psychology of Women's Experience.* New York: Basic Books, 1992.

Keane, Philip. *Sexual Morality: A Catholic Perspective.* New York: Paulist Press, 1978.

Keen, Sam. *The Passionate Life.* San Francisco: Harper & Row, 1983.

Keenan, James. *Virtues for Ordinary Christians.* Franklin, Wis.: Sheed & Ward, 1999.

Kehrwald, Lief. *Marriage and the Spirituality of Intimacy.* Cincinnati, Oh.: St. Anthony Messenger Press, 1997.

Kelsey, Morton, and Barbara Kelsey. *Sacrament of Sexuality.* Warwick, N.Y.: Amity House, 1986.

Kennedy, Eugene. *The Unhealed Wound: The Church and Human Sexuality.* New York: St. Martins Press, 2001.

Koch, Carl, and Joyce Heil. *Created in God's Image: Meditating on Our Body.* Winona, Minn.: Saint Mary's Press, 1991.

Koch, Patricia, and David Weis. *Sexuality in America: Understanding Our Sexual Values and Behavior.* New York: Continuum, 1999.

Koller, Alice. *The Stations of Solitude.* New York: Bantam Books, 1990.

Kooden, Harold. *Golden Men: The Power of Gay Midlife.* New York: Avon Books, 2000.

Kosnik, Anthony, et al. *Human Sexuality: New Directions in American Catholic Thought.* New York: Paulist Press, 1977.

Kotre, John. *Making It Count: How to Generate a Legacy That Gives Meaning to Your Life.* New York: Free Press, 1999.

———. *Outliving the Self.* Baltimore: Johns Hopkins University Press, 1984.

Kunz, George. *The Paradox of Power and Weakness: Levinas and an Alternative Paradigm for Psychology.* Albany: State University of New York Press, 1998.

LaCugna, Catherine Mowry, ed. *Freeing Theology: The Essentials of Theology in Feminist Perspective.* San Francisco: HarperSan Francisco, 1993.

Laumann, Edward, and Robert Michael, eds. *Sex, Love and Health in America: Private Choices and Public Policy.* Chicago: University of Chicago Press, 2000.

Lebacqz, Karen. "Appropriate Vulnerability: A Sexual Ethic for Singles." In *Sexuality: A Reader,* edited by Karen Lebacqz and David Sinacore-Guinn. New York: Pilgrim Press, 2001.

Lerner, Harriet Goldhor. *The Dance of Intimacy.* New York: Harper Collins, 1990.

Levant, Robert, and Gary Brooks, eds. *Men and Sex: New Psychological Perspectives.* New York: John Wiley, 1997.

Liuzzi, Peter J. *With Listening Hearts: Understanding the Voices of Lesbian and Gay Catholics.* New York: Paulist Press, 2001.

Logue, Judy. *Forgiving the People You Love to Hate.* Liguori, Mo.: Liguori Press, 1997.

Maccoby, Eleanor E. *The Two Sexes: Growing Apart, Coming Together.* Cambridge, Mass.: Belnap Press, 1999.

Maclean, Norman. *A River Runs Through It.* Chicago: University of Chicago Press, 1992.

Mahoney, John. *The Making of Moral Theology.* New York: Oxford University Press, 1989.

Martini, Cardinal Carlo Maria. *On the Body: A Contemporary Theology of Sexuality.* New York: Crossroad, 2000.

McAdams, Dan, and Edward de St. Aubin, eds. *Generativity and Adult Development.* Washington, D.C.: American Psychological Association, 1998.

McCary, James. *Human Sexuality.* 3rd edition. New York: Van Nostrand, 1978.

McDonald, Patrick, and Claudette McDonald. *Marital Spirituality: The Search for the Hidden Ground of Love.* New York: Paulist Press, 1999.

McNamara, Jo Ann. *A New Song: Celibate Women in the First Three Christian Centuries.* New York: Hawthorne Press, 1985.

McNeill, John. *Both Feet Firmly Planted in Mid-Air: My Spiritual Journey.* Philadelphia: Westminster John Knox, 1998.

Miller, Jean Baker. *Toward a New Psychology of Women.* Boston: Beacon Press, 1986.

Miller, Patricia Martens. *Sex is Not a Four-Letter Word: Talking Sex with Your Children Made Easier.* New York: Crossroad, 1995.

Moltmann-Wendel, Elizabeth. *I Am My Body: A Theology of Embodiment.* New York: Continuum, 1995.

Montague, Ashley. *Touching: The Human Significance of Skin.* 2nd edition. San Francisco: Harper & Row, 1978.

Moore, Thomas. *The Soul of Sex: Cultivating Life as an Act of Love.* New York: HarperCollins, 1999.

Muller-Fahrenholz, Geiko. *The Art of Forgiveness: Theological Reflections on Healing and Reconciliation.* New York: World Council of Churches, 1997.

Murphy, Roland. "Commentary on Song of Songs." In *The Jerome Biblical Commentary,* edited by Raymond E. Brown, Joseph A. Fitzmyer, and Roland E. Murphy. New York: Prentice-Hall, 1968.

Nardi, Peter. *Men's Friendships: Research on Men and Masculinities.* New York: Sage Publications, 1992.

National Conference of Catholic Bishops. "Always Our Children: A Pastoral Message to Parents of Homosexual Children and Suggestions for Pastoral Ministers." Washington, D.C.: United States Catholic Conference, 1998.

———. "Follow The Way of Love: A Pastoral Message to Families." Washington, D.C.: United States Catholic Conference, 1993.

———. "Human Sexuality: A Catholic Perspective for Education and Lifelong Learning." Washington, D.C.: United States Catholic Conference, 1991.

Nelson, James. *Body Theology.* Philadelphia: Westminster John Knox, 1992.

———. *Embodiment: An Approach to Sexuality and Christian Theology.* Minneapolis: Augsburg, 1990.

———. *The Intimate Connection: Male Sexuality, Masculine Spirituality.* Philadelphia: Westminster John Knox, 1991.

———. "Reuniting Sexuality and Spirituality." *Christian Century* (February 25, 1987).

———, and Sandra Longfellow, eds. *Sexuality and the Sacred: Sources for Theological Reflection.* Philadelphia: Westminster John Knox Press, 1994.

Neuger, Christie Cozad, and James Newton Poling, eds. *The Care of Men.* Nashville: Abingdon, 1997.

Newman, John Cardinal. *On Consulting the Faithful in Matters of Doctrine.* New York: Sheed & Ward, 1961.

Nicholson, John. *Men and Women: How Different Are They?* 2nd edition. New York: Oxford University Press, 1993.

Nugent, Robert, and Jeannine Gramick. *Building Bridges: Gay and Lesbian Reality and the Catholic Church.* Mystic, Conn.: Twenty-Third Publications, 1992.

Nussbaum, Martha. *Women and Human Development: The Capabilities Approach.* New York: Cambridge University Press, 2000.

Oliver, Mary Anne. *Conjugal Spirituality: The Primacy of Mutual Love in Christian Tradition.* Franklin, Wis.: Sheed & Ward, 2000.

O'Murchu, Diarmuid. *Poverty, Celibacy, and Obedience: A Radical Option for Life.* New York: Crossroad, 1999.

O'Neill, Craig. *Coming Out Within: Stages of Spiritual Awakening for Lesbians and Gay Men.* San Francisco: HarperSanFrancisco, 1992.

Perito, John. *Sexuality and Faith: A Psychiatric Approach.* New York: Crossroad, 2001.

Perkins, Pheme. *Love Commands in the New Testament.* New York: Paulist Press, 1982.

Phillips, Adam. *On Kissing, Tickling, and Being Bored.* Cambridge, Mass.: Harvard University Press, 1993.

Pogrebin, Letty Cottin. *Among Friends.* New York: McGraw-Hill, 1987.

Pollack, William. *Real Boys: Rescuing Our Sons from the Myths of Boyhood.* New York: Holt, 1998.

———, and Ronald Levant, eds. *A New Psychology of Men.* New York: Basic Books, 1995.

Rolheiser, Ronald. *The Holy Longing: The Search for a Christian Spirituality.* New York: Doubleday, 1999.

Ross, Susan. *Extravagant Affections.* New York: Continuum, 1998.

Rossi, Alice. *Caring and Doing for Others.* Chicago: University of Chicago Press, 2001.

Rubin, Lillian. *Just Friends.* New York: Harper & Row, 1985.

———. *Tangled Lives: Daughters, Mothers and the Crucible of Aging.* Boston: Beacon Press, 2000.

Sammon, Sean D. *The Undivided Heart: Making Sense of Celibate Chastity.* Staten Island, N.Y.: Alba House, 1993.

Sang, Barbara, Joyce Warshov, and Adrienne Smith. *Lesbians at Midlife: The Creative Transition.* Minneapolis: Spinster Ink, 1991.

Scarf, Maggie. *Intimate Partners: Patterns in Love and Marriage.* New York: Ballantine Books, 1996.

Schillebeeckx, Edward. *Marriage: Human Reality and Saving Mystery.* London: Sheed & Ward, 1999.

———. *Ministry.* New York: Crossroad, 1981.

Schnarch, David. *Passionate Marriage: Love, Sex and Intimacy in Emotionally Committed Relationships.* New York: Henry Holt, 1998.

Schneiders, Sandra. *Finding the Treasure: Locating Catholic Religious Life in a New Ecclesial and Cultural Context.* New York: Paulist Press, 2000.

————. *Selling All: Commitment, Consecrated Celibacy and Community in Catholic Religious Life.* New York: Paulist Press, 2001.

Schreiter, Robert. *The Ministry of Reconciliation: Spirituality and Strategies.* Maryknoll, N.Y.: Orbis Books, 1998.

Scott, Kieran, and Michael Warren, eds. *Perspectives on Marriage: A Reader.* 2nd edition. New York: Oxford University Press, 2000.

Sheehy, Sandy. *Connecting: The Enduring Power of Women's Friendship.* New York: William Morrow, 2000.

Shelton, Robert. *Loving Relationships.* Elgin, Ill.: Brethren Press, 1987.

Sheridan, Jean. *The Unwilling Celibate: A Spirituality for Single Adults.* Mystic, Conn.: Twenty-Third Publishers, 2000.

Shinnick, Maurice. *This Remarkable Gift: Being Gay and Catholic.* New York: Paul & Company Publishing, 1998.

Sipe, Richard. *Celibacy: A Way of Loving, Living, and Serving.* New York: Triumph Books, 1996.

St. Camille, Mark, and Lou Moretti. *It's Okay to Be Single.* New York: It's Okay Publishing, 2000.

Stoltz, Eric. "Notes From a Community–Catholic and Gay." *America* (March 28, 1998).

Stone Center. "Works in Progress." Wellesley Centers for Women, Wellesley, MA 02181-8268.

Stuart, Elizabeth. *Just Good Friends: Toward a Lesbian and Gay Theology of Relationships.* London: Mowbray, 1995.

Sullivan, Andrew. "Alone Again, Naturally." *The New Republic* (November 28,1994).

————. *Love Undetectable: Notes on Friendship, Sex, and Survival.* New York: Vintage, 1999.

Tannen, Deborah. *I Only Say This Because I Love You: How the Way We Talk Can Make or Break Relationships.* New York: Random House, 2001.

————. *You Just Don't Understand: Women and Men in Conversation.* New York: Ballantine Books, 1991.

Tarvis, Cheryl Brown, and Jacquelyn W. White, eds. *Sexuality, Society, and Feminism.* Washington, D.C.: American Psychological Association, 1999.

Tavris, Carol. *The Mismeasure of Women.* New York: Simon & Schuster, 1993.

Taylor, Jill, Carol Gilligan, and Amy Sullivan. *Between Voice and Silence:*

Women and Girls, Race and Relationship. Cambridge, Mass.: Harvard University Press, 1995.

Thomas Aquinas. *Summa Contra Gentiles.* Translated by Vernon J. Bourke and Charles J. O'Neill. Notre Dame, Ind.: Notre Dame Press, 1975.

Timmerman, Joan. *Sexuality and Spiritual Growth.* New York: Crossroad, 1992.

Traina, Christine. "Papal Ideals, Marital Realities: One View from the Ground." In *Sexual Diversity and Catholicism,* edited by Patricia Beattie Jung with Joseph Coray. Collegeville, Minn.: Liturgical Press, 2001.

Unger, Roberto. *Passion: An Essay on Personality.* New York: Free Press, 1984.

Vogels, Heinz. *Celibacy: Gift or Law?* Franklin, Wis.: Sheed & Ward, 1999.

Voist, Judith. *Suddenly Sixty.* New York: Simon & Schuster, 2000.

Wallace, Catherine Miles. *For Fidelity: How Intimacy and Commitment Enrich Our Lives.* New York: Knopf, 1999.

Wallerstein, Judith, and Sandra Blakeslee. *Good Marriage: How and Why Love Lasts.* New York: Warner Books, 1996.

Westley, Dick. *A Theology of Presence.* Mystic, Conn.: Twenty-Third Publishers, 1989.

———. *Morality and Its Beyond.* Mystic, Conn.: Twenty-Third Publishers, 1984.

Whitehead, Evelyn Eaton, and James D. Whitehead. *Christian Life Patterns: Psychological Challenges and Religious Invitations of Adult Life.* New York: Crossroad, 1994.

———. *Community of Faith: Crafting Christian Communities Today.* Mystic, Conn.: Twenty-Third Publishers, 1993.

———. *Marrying Well: Stages on the Journey of Christian Marriage.* New York: Doubleday, 1983.

Whitehead, James D., and Evelyn Eaton. *The Promise of Partnership: A Model for Collaborative Ministry.* Lincoln, Neb.: iUniverse.com Publishers, 2000.

———. *Seasons of Strength: New Visions of Adult Christian Maturing.* Winona, Minn.: Saint Mary's Press, 1996.

Wink, Walter, ed. *Homosexuality and Christian Faith: Questions of Concience for the Church.* Minneapolis: Fortress Press, 1999.